Anonymus

The Book of Hours

In which are contained offices for the seven canonical hours, litanies, and other

devotions

Anonymus

The Book of Hours
In which are contained offices for the seven canonical hours, litanies, and other devotions

ISBN/EAN: 9783742821737

Manufactured in Europe, USA, Canada, Australia, Japa

Cover: Foto ©Andreas Hilbeck / pixelio.de

Manufactured and distributed by brebook publishing software (www.brebook.com)

Anonymus

The Book of Hours

THE Book of Hours

IN WHICH ARE CONTAINED

OFFICES FOR THE SEVEN CANONICAL
HOURS, LITANIES, AND OTHER
DEVOTIONS

> "Seven times a day do I praise Thee
> Because of Thy righteous judgments."
> Ps. cxix. 164.

NEW YORK
PUBLISHED BY HURD AND HOUGHTON
BOSTON: E. P. DUTTON AND COMPANY
1866

THE CONTENTS OF THIS BOOK.

	PAGE
THE PREFACE	5
THE OFFICES FOR THE SEVEN CANONICAL HOURS	18
THE PROPER SERVICE OF THE SEASON	51
THE PSALTER OF THE HOURS	78
THE LITANIES	107
THE COLLECTS, PRAYERS, AND OTHER DEVOTIONS	121
THE HYMNS	189

PREFACE.

THIS book was prepared for a special purpose. It has pleased Almighty GOD, within the last few years, to put into the hearts of some among us the desire to serve Him with a devotion hitherto unknown in our own communion. These persons, so called of the Holy Ghost to give themselves up to charitable and religious works, and, as the Apostle expresses it, " to continue in supplications and prayers night and day," have sought and embraced the life of a Community, as the only one in which their desire towards GOD can be satisfied. Among the blessed and unspeakable privileges of such a life of retirement from this world and its affairs is that of being able to use and regularly observe the Seven Hours of Prayer. This little volume is intended to aid in such observance. The work of its preparation was undertaken in compliance with earnest requests on the part of some who felt the need of such assistance as it might give; and, although, to some extent, it may be used with profit by others less privileged than they, it should be judged of by its design, and estimated according to the mission which it was intended to fulfil. It is not a "Manual of Devotions" in the general acceptation of that term; the plan of such a Manual has already been drawn, and may at some time, if GOD will, be filled up by the

PREFACE.

writer, in hope of furnishing a work suited to tne faithful members of our Church, at large; but this Book of Hours is simply what it professes to be, and is intended only for such as keep the Hours, with more or less regularity and constancy, according to the circumstances of their life, and especially for those already mentioned as being able to walk in that narrower way, which our Blessed Master has been pleased to open to their willing feet.

The use and observance of the Hours is a practice which needs no argument to recommend it and no apology to justify it. The Holy Scriptures suggest it, and Catholic Tradition, commends it to all devout people. "Seven times a day do I praise Thee," said the Psalmist of Israel. And again, "in the evening and morning and at noonday will I pray, and that instantly;" and, "at midnight will I rise to give thanks unto Thee." Such resolves cannot be habitually entertained in the heart without finding a practical method of fulfilment. How old this use is we do not know; it must be very ancient. The Jews were familiar with it; the holy Apostles practised it. "Peter and John went up to the temple at the hour of prayer, being the ninth hour." At the third hour of the day, on Pentecost, "they were all with one accord in one place." About the sixth hour Peter went up upon the house-top to pray; and it was at the ninth hour that Cornelius saw in a vision the angel of GOD. At midnight Paul and Silas prayed and sang praises unto GOD in the prison. When we consider the practice of reciting the Offices of the Hours, as it has been continued all along in the Catholic Church, Eastern and Western alike, and then, reverting to the records of the Apostolic days, trace up the subject towards the remoter ages which preceded them, we must hold it to be, substantially, one of those observances to which the memory of Man runneth not contrary. Meanwhile we cannot but be struck by the variety of the ends which it has been thought to aim at. "It is a memorial of the seven days of Creation; it is an honor done to the seven petitions given to us by our Lord in His prayer; it is a mode of pleading for the influence of that Spirit who is revealed to us as sevenfold in His gifts; on the other hand it is a preservative against those seven evil spirits, which are apt to return to the exorcised soul, more wicked than he who has been driven out of it, and it was a fit remedy of those seven successive falls which the Scripture says happen to the just man daily."

We think it to be impossible to compose a Liturgy; for a Liturgy is a growth, a production of long years, the result of centuries of practice. Not less impossible would it be to compose, *de novo*, a Book of Hours. Any person possessing the requisite intelligence and cultivation might construct original offices of prayer adapted to the canonical times of the day; but the work so made up would not stand the test of constant reciting. The compilers of our Book of Common Prayer knew this full well, and therefore they drew on the ancient treasures, framing the order for Daily Morning Prayer from the offices for Matins, Lauds, and Prime then in use, and that for Daily Evening Prayer from the offices for Vespers and Compline. This volume has been made up in the same way, after a collation of many offices, Anglican, Gallican, and Oriental. We can go to no other sources for our spiritual food, without encountering the weak devices of man. There is in the Creeds, Hymns, Collects, and Lit-

PREFACE.

anies of the Holy Catholic Church a secondary inspiration which places them beyond all human productions; this alone can explain their perpetual freshness and power. Offices must be framed of those materials, if it is hoped that they will satisfy the soul and serve the need of years.

The Seven Times of Prayer, according to immemorial tradition, are as follows. The 1st is that portion of the twenty-four hours when, midnight being past, it is still dark, but drawing towards the day. The Offices used at that time were known as Nocturns and Matins; the Nocturns being divided into three parts, known respectively as the 1st, 2d, and 3d Nocturn, and the Matins, which followed immediately upon the Nocturns, being prolonged and terminated in an Office called Lauds, which was said at daybreak. The 2d time is that of the sunrising, at which the office known as Prime, and corresponding to Early Morning prayer was used. The 3d time is nine o'clock A. M., the "third hour of the day" in a double sense; it was then that our Blessed Lord was devoted to Crucifixion by His foes, and at that hour the Holy Ghost descended on the Day of Pentecost. The 4th time is twelve o'clock meridian, at which period the Lord was hanging on the cross, and the darkness was gathering upon the land. At three P. M. is said the 5th Office, in commemoration of our Redeemer's death, and with special remembrance of those in the agony of their own dissolution, or approaching it. The hour of Vespers comes with the fall of the evening; and 7thly and lastly, is said the Compline Office, when it is dark once more, and when the night-watches are again begun.

In arranging the services for these consecrated Times,

PREFACE.

the following objects were had in view by the compiler of this book: —

1st. To make the Offices as brief as was consistent with the purposes to be served, — the glorifying of GOD, and the edification of the souls of the faithful.

2dly. To adhere to the form and spirit of the ancient Offices.

3dly. To give as much flexibility as possible.

4thly. To avoid unnecessary complexity of arrangement.

As to flexibility, it will be found by the student that there is in this respect a great difference between the Anglican and Gallican Hours, and a difference still more marked between the forms used respectively in the Eastern and Western branches of the Church. The Gallican type has been followed by the compiler, especially in the arrangement of the Psalter; and they who have been accustomed to use the "Day Hours of the Church of England," or similar works which might be referred to, will at once observe the variations, particularly as it relates to the use of the 119th Psalm at four out of the Seven Offices daily throughout the entire year; this is a peculiarity of the Books in use in England, but is not found in the Gallican Offices. The Oriental Offices are so peculiar in structure and contents, that it was deemed inadvisable to attempt a combination of them with the Western Offices; they have furnished, however, some beautiful prayers, and at least one hymn, as familiar in the East as is *Magnificat* in the West.

A Book of Hours must, from the nature of the case, be complicated; it will be more or less so in proportion to its fulness. Not but that it would be practicable to arrange seven Offices, to be read straight through without variation or change; nothing would be easier to do. But to use those forms, every day, three hundred and sixty-five times each in every year, without reference to changes of the Calendar, would be more than human nature could endure. There must be variety, and that variety must extend to the five great seasons, Advent, Christmas Tide, Lent, Easter Tide, and the Trinity season. The more numerous the changes, and the more characteristic of each leading mystery of Redemption as successively presented, the more satisfactory will be the Offices. It is, however, impossible to attain this very desirable end without a degree of complication in arrangement, or an enormous expenditure of space in repetition of the forms employed. Some degree of complexity was inevitable; but it is believed that an examination and study of half an hour will enable any one accustomed to the Book of Common Prayer to use this little manual without difficulty.

A few words, in addition, on certain points of practice.

These Offices may be used, either privately or in community. When used in private, they should be read through, the person saying versicles and responses alike in full. When used in community, some one must act as Reader; after secret prayer, all present should rise, and the Reader should begin with the invocation of the Blessed Trinity, to which all reply, Amen. The Office is continued all standing until the words, " Let us pray," at which all kneel and so remain until the end; the Reader always saying whatever is marked ℣., and the persons present always making the responses marked ℟.; thus, there is but one change of posture throughout.

In the use of the Collects, Litanies, and Hymns, it is

PREFACE.

intended that the greatest freedom should be exercised, the Reader appointing hymns at discretion, and using prayers as occasion requires or circumstances suggest. The Litanies may be substituted for the Offices, at pleasure, or added to them.

Wherever the privilege of the Daily Service may be had, the order for Morning and Evening Prayer would, of course, take the place of the Prime and Vesper Offices; and on Sundays, only the Matins and Compline Offices would be required, if the full services of the Church were duly said.

That the Blessed Head of the Church will graciously accept this work and sanctify it through His intercession to the good of His People, is the humble prayer of one, who, less than the least of His servants, finds nothing of his own to give, but everything to ask from the indulgence of his brethren and the Mercy of the Master.

NEW YORK. *Easter Tide.* 1865.

I.

THE OFFICES

FOR THE

SEVEN CANONICAL HOURS.

L

OFFICE FOR MATINS.

IN the Name of the Father and of the Son and of the Holy Ghost. *Amen.*

Our Father, who art in heaven, Hallowed be thy Name. Thy kingdom come. Thy will be done on earth, As it is in heaven. Give us this day our daily bread. And forgive us our trespasses, as we forgive those who trespass against us. And lead us not into temptation; But deliver us from evil: For thine is the kingdom, and the power, and the glory, for ever and ever. *Amen.*

℣. O Lord, open Thou our lips.

℟. And our mouth shall show forth Thy praise.

¶ *Then shall be said, at certain seasons, a ℣. and ℟., as follows:*

During Advent, daily.

℣. Send, O Lord, the Lamb to the Ruler of the Land.

℟. From Sela to the wilderness, unto the mount of the daughter of Zion.

During Christmas Tide, daily.

℣. The Word was made Flesh. Alleluia.

℟. And dwelt among us. Alleluia.

During Lent, daily.

℣. Draw nigh unto my soul and save it.

℟. O deliver me because of mine enemies.

During Easter Tide, daily.

℣. In Thy Resurrection, O Christ.

℟. Let heaven and earth rejoice.

On Sundays and Feast Days, at all other times throughout the year.

℣. The Lord is high above all people.

℟. And His glory above the heavens.

¶ *Then shall the Office proceed as follows:*

℣. O God, make speed to save us.

℟. O Lord, make haste to help us.

℣. Glory be to the Father, and to the Son, and to the Holy Ghost.

℟. As it was in the beginning, is now, and ever shall be, world without end. *Amen.*

Alleluia!

¶ *But from Septuagesima Sunday to Wednesday in Holy Week, inclusive, is said instead:*

Praise to Thee, O Lord, we sing,
Of glory the Eternal King.

15

OFFICE FOR MATINS.

¶ *Then shall be said the Psalms for the day from the Psalter of the Hours.*

¶ *Then shall follow the Chapter, Rev. vii. 12, with ℟., from Epiphany to Septuagesima, and from Trinity Monday to Advent, but at all other times the Chapter shall be taken from the proper Service of the Season.*

Blessing, and glory, and wisdom, and thanksgiving, and honor, and power, and might, be unto our God for ever and ever. *Amen.*

℟. Thanks be to God.

¶ *Then shall be sung the following hymn, or that in the Service of the Season.*

Iam lucis orto sidere.

NOW that the daylight fills the sky,
We lift our hearts to God on high,
That He, in all we do or say,
Would keep us safe from harm this day.

Would guard our hearts and tongues from strife,
From anger's din would shield our life,
From all ill sights would turn our eyes,
Would close our ears from vanities.

Would keep our inmost conscience pure,
Our souls from folly would secure,
Would bid us check the pride of sense
With due and holy abstinence.

So we, when this new day is gone,
And night in turn is drawing on,
With conscience by the world unstained,
Shall praise His Name for victory gained.

All laud to God the Father be,
All laud, Eternal Son, to Thee,
All laud as is for ever meet,
To God the Holy Paraclete.
Amen.

¶ *Then shall follow the Prayers.*

℣. The Lord be with you.

℟. And with thy spirit.

Let us pray.

℣. Lord, be merciful unto me.

℟. Heal my soul, for I have sinned against Thee.

℣. Turn Thee again, O Lord, at the last.

℟. And be gracious unto Thy servants.

℣. Let thy merciful kindness, O Lord, be upon us.

℟. As we do put our trust in Thee.

℣. Let Thy priests be clothed with righteousness.

℟. And Thy saints sing with joyfulness.

℣. O Lord, save the people of this nation.

℟. And mercifully hear us when we call upon Thee.

℣. O God, save Thy servants and handmaidens.

℟. Which put their trust in Thee.

℣. Let us pray for the peace of Jerusalem.

℟. Peace be within thy walls, and plenteousness within thy palaces.

℣. Lord, hear our prayer.

℟. And let our cry come unto Thee.

16

OFFICE FOR MATINS.

¶ *Then shall be said the Collect for the day, and after that any other Collects and devotions; after which, on Sundays and Feast Days, shall be said the Memorials as follows.*

Memorial of the Incarnation of our Lord.

(*This is not to be said from Maunday Thursday to Low Sunday, inclusive.*)

Antiphon. Lo, Mary hath brought forth the Saviour, of whom, when John saw Him, he said, Behold the Lamb of God, which taketh away the sin of the world.

℣. Thou art fairer than the children of men.

℟. Full of grace are Thy lips.

THE COLLECT.

WE beseech thee, O Lord, pour Thy grace into our hearts; that as we have known the incarnation of Thy Son Jesus Christ, by the message of an angel; so by His cross and passion we may be brought unto the glory of His resurrection, through the same Jesus Christ our Lord. *Amen.*

Memorial of All Saints.

(*Not said from Maunday Thursday to Low Sunday.*)

Antiphon. Behold the Lord my God shall come, and all His Saints with Him, and there shall be in that day a great light.

℣. The souls of the righteous are in the hand of God.

℟. And there shall no torment touch them.

THE COLLECT.

O ALMIGHTY GOD, who hast knit together Thine elect in one communion and fellowship, in the mystical body of Thy Son Christ our Lord; grant us grace so to follow Thy blessed saints in all virtuous and godly living, that we may come to those unspeakable joys which Thou hast prepared for those who unfeignedly love Thee, through Jesus Christ our Lord. *Amen.*

Memorial of the Passion.

(*To be said from Trinity Sunday to Advent.*)

Antiphon. It behoveth us to glory in the Cross of our Lord Jesus Christ.

℣. All the world shall worship Thee, O God.

℟. Sing of Thee, and praise Thy power.

THE COLLECT.

KEEP, we beseech Thee, O Saviour of the world, in continual peace, those whom Thou hast been pleased to redeem by Thy Cross and Passion, who livest and reignest with the Father and the Holy Ghost, one God, world without end. *Amen.*

¶ *Matins shall then and always be concluded as follows.*

℣. The Lord be with you.
℟. And with thy spirit.
℣. Bless we the Lord.
℟. Thanks be to God.

The Almighty and merciful God, the Father, Son, and Holy Ghost, bless and keep us, now and for ever. *Amen.*

II.

OFFICE FOR PRIME OR FIRST HOUR.

7 O'clock A. M.

IN the Name of the Father, &c.

Our Father, &c.

I believe in God the Father Almighty, Maker of heaven and earth:

And in Jesus Christ his only Son our Lord; Who was conceived by the Holy Ghost, Born of the Virgin Mary; Suffered under Pontius Pilate, Was crucified, dead, and buried; He descended into hell, The third day he rose from the dead; He ascended into heaven, And sitteth on the right hand of God the Father Almighty; From thence He shall come to judge the quick and the dead.

I believe in the Holy Ghost; The holy Catholic Church, The Communion of Saints; the Forgiveness of sins; The Resurrection of the body; And the Life everlasting. *Amen.*

℣. O God, make speed, &c.

℟. O Lord, make haste, &c.

℣. Glory be to the Father, &c.

℟. As it was in the beginning, &c.

℣. Praise ye the Lord.

℟. The Lord's Name be praised.

¶ *Then shall be sung the following, or any other hymn.*

Omnis fidelis gaudeat.

I.

LET every faithful heart rejoice,
And render thanks to God on high;
And with each power of soul and voice,
Extol His praises worthily.

II.

Into this dark world Jesus came,
And all men might His Form behold;
While to the limits of the same
He passed, that we might be consoled.

III.

To all He showed that gentle Face;
On good and bad alike it shone;
Its perfect loveliness and grace,
The Lord of all concealed from none.

IV.

O love of Christ beyond all love!
O clemency beyond all thought!
O grace all praise of men above,
Whereby such gifts to men are brought!

OFFICE FOR PRIME, OR FIRST HOUR.

v.

O Blessed Lord whose praise we sing!
Here in the way we worship Thee:
That in the country of our King
Filled with thy glory we may be.

vi.

To God on high be glory meet,
Equal to Thee, Eternal Son,
Equal to Thee, Blest Paraclete,
While never-ending ages run.
Amen.

¶ *Immediately after the hymn shall be said the ℣. and ℟. for the season.*

In Advent, daily —

℣. Behold our King cometh.

℟. Let us go forth to meet the Saviour.

In Christmas Tide —

℣. Christ is born unto us.

℟. O come, let us adore.

Epiphany to Septuagesima —

℣. Let us come before the Face of the Lord.

℟. And with psalms rejoice before Him.

In Easter Tide —

℣. Alleluia, Alleluia! Christ is risen.

℟. The Lord is risen indeed, and hath appeared unto Simon. Alleluia, Alleluia!

Ascension Day to Whitsunday —

℣. Christ, ascending into heaven,

℟. O come, let us adore.

Whitsunday to Trinity Sunday —

℣. The Spirit of the Lord hath filled the orb of the world.

℟. O come, let us adore.

On Trinity Sunday, only —

℣. The one God in Trinity and Trinity in Unity,

℟. O come, let us adore.

Trinity Monday to Advent —

℣. The Lord open our hearts in His law.

℟. And in His precepts give us peace.

¶ *Then shall be said the Psalms for Prime, as appointed in the Psalter of the Hours.*

¶ *Then shall be said the Chapter.*

On Sundays and Feast Days throughout the year, 1 Tim. i. 17.

Now unto the King, eternal, immortal, invisible, the only wise God, be honor and glory for ever and ever. *Amen.*

On all other days, 1 St. John, i.

If we walk in the light, as He is in the light, we have fellowship one with another, and the Blood of Jesus Christ His Son cleanseth us from all sin.

¶ *After the chapter, and after every chapter wherever it occurs, shall be said —*

℣. But Thou, O Lord, have mercy upon us.

℟. Thanks be to God.

¶ *Then shall be sung a Canticle, as follows:*

On Sundays and Feast Days, Benedictus. St. Luke, i. 68.

BLESSED be the Lord God of Israel: for He hath visited and redeemed His people:
And hath raised up a mighty salvation for us: in the house of His servant David.
As He spake by the mouth of

OFFICE FOR PRIME, OR FIRST HOUR.

His holy prophets: which have been since the world began;

That we should be saved from our enemies: and from the hand of all that hate us;

To perform the mercy promised to our forefathers: and to remember His holy covenant;

To perform the oath which He sware to our forefather Abraham: that He would give us;

That we, being delivered out of the hand of our enemies: might serve Him without fear;

In holiness and righteousness before Him: all the days of our life.

And thou, child, shalt be called the Prophet of the Highest: for thou shalt go before the face of the Lord to prepare His ways;

To give knowledge of salvation unto His people: for the remission of their sins;

Through the tender mercy of our God: whereby the Dayspring from on high hath visited us;

To give light to them that sit in darkness and in the shadow of death: and to guide our feet into the way of peace.

Glory be to the Father, &c.

On Mondays, the Song of Isaiah, chap. xii. Confitebor tibi.

O LORD, I will praise Thee, though Thou wast angry with me: Thine anger is turned away, and Thou comfortedst me.

Behold, God is my salvation; I will trust and not be afraid: for the Lord Jehovah is my strength and my song, He also is become my salvation.

Therefore with joy shall ye draw water out of the wells of salvation: and in that day shall ye say, Praise the Lord, call upon His Name;

Declare His doings among the people: make mention that His Name is exalted.

Sing unto the Lord, for He hath done excellent things: this is known in all the earth.

Cry out and shout, thou inhabitant of Zion: for great is the Holy One of Israel in the midst of thee.

Glory be to the Father, &c.

On Tuesdays, the Song of Hezekiah: Isaiah xxxviii. 10. Ego dixi in dimidio.

I SAID in the cutting off of my days: I shall go to the gates of the grave.

I am deprived of the residue of my years: I said, I shall not see the Lord, even the Lord, in the land of the living.

I shall behold man no more: with the inhabitants of the world.

Mine age is departed: and is removed from me as a shepherd's tent.

I have cut off like a weaver my life: he will cut me off with pining sickness.

From day even to night: wilt thou make an end of me.

I reckoned till morning that as a lion so will he break all my bones: from day even to night wilt Thou make an end of me.

Like a crane or a swallow, so did I chatter: I did mourn as a dove.

Mine eyes fail with looking upward: O Lord, I am oppressed, undertake for me.

What shall I say? He hath both spoken unto me, and Him-

OFFICE FOR PRIME, OR FIRST HOUR.

self hath done it: I shall go softly all my years in the bitterness of my soul.

O Lord, by these things men live, and in all these things is the life of my spirit: so wilt Thou recover me and make me to live.

Behold, for peace I had great bitterness; but Thou hast in love to my soul delivered it from the pit of corruption: for Thou hast cast all my sins behind Thy back.

For the grave cannot praise Thee, death cannot celebrate Thee: they that go down to the pit cannot hope for Thy truth.

The living, the living, he shall praise Thee as I do this day; the father to the children shall make known Thy truth.

The Lord was ready to save me: therefore we will sing my songs to the stringed instruments all the days of our life in the house of the Lord.

Glory be to the Father, &c.

On Wednesdays, the Song of Hannah: 1 Samuel ii. 1. Exultavit cor meum.

MY heart rejoiceth in the Lord: mine horn is exalted in the Lord.

My mouth is enlarged over mine enemies: because I rejoice in Thy salvation.

There is none holy as the Lord, for there is none beside Thee: neither is there any rock like our God.

Talk no more exceeding proudly: let not arrogancy come out of your mouth.

For the Lord is a God of knowledge: and by Him actions are weighed.

The bows of the mighty men are broken: and they that stumbled are girded with strength.

They that were full have hired out themselves for bread: and they that were hungry ceased.

So that the barren hath borne seven: and she that hath many children is waxed feeble.

The Lord killeth and maketh alive: He bringeth down to the grave and bringeth up.

The Lord maketh poor and maketh rich, He bringeth low and lifteth up: He raiseth up the poor out of the dust, and lifteth up the beggar from the dunghill.

To set them among princes: and to make them inherit the throne of glory.

For the pillars of the earth are the Lord's: and He hath set the world upon them.

He will keep the feet of His saints, and the wicked shall be silent in darkness: for by strength shall no man prevail.

The adversaries of the Lord shall be broken in pieces: out of heaven shall He thunder upon them.

The Lord shall judge the ends of the earth, and He shall give strength unto His king: and exalt the horn of His anointed.

Glory be to the Father, &c.

On Thursdays, the Song in the Land of Judah: Isaiah xxvi. 1. Urbs fortitudinis.

We have a strong city: salvation will God appoint for walls and bulwarks.

Open ye the gates: that the righteous nation which keepeth the truth may enter in.

Thou wilt keep him in perfect peace whose mind is stayed on

OFFICE FOR PRIME, OR FIRST HOUR.

Thee: because he trusteth in Thee.

Trust ye in the Lord forever: for in the Lord Jehovah is everlasting strength.

For He bringeth down them that dwell on high: the lofty city, He layeth it low.

He layeth it low even to the ground: He bringeth it even to the dust.

The foot shall tread it down: even the feet of the poor, and the steps of the needy.

The way of the just is uprightness: Thou, most upright, dost weigh the path of the just.

Yea, in the way of Thy judgments, O Lord, have we waited for Thee: the desire of our soul is to Thy Name, and to the remembrance of Thee.

With my soul have I desired Thee in the night: yea, with my spirit within me will I seek Thee early.

Glory be to the Father, &c.

On Fridays, Ecclus. xxxix. 13.
Obaudite me.

Hearken unto me, ye holy children: and bud forth as a rose growing by the brook of the field.

And give ye a sweet savour as frankincense, and flourish as a lily: sing a song of praise, bless the Lord in all His works.

Magnify His Name: and show forth His praise with the songs of your lips, and with harps.

And in praising Him ye shall say after this manner: All the works of the Lord are exceeding good.

At His commandment the waters stood as an heap: and at the words of His mouth the receptacles of waters.

At His commandment is done whatsoever pleaseth Him: and none can hinder when He will save.

The works of all flesh are before Him: and nothing can be hid from His eyes.

He seeth from everlasting to everlasting: and there is nothing wonderful before Him.

All the works of the Lord are good: and He will give every needful thing in due season.

Glory be to the Father, &c.

On Saturdays, the Prayer of Jonah: ii. 8.

I cried by reason of my affliction unto the Lord, and He heard me: out of the belly of hell cried I, and Thou heardest my voice.

For Thou hadst cast me into the deep, in the midst of the seas, and the floods compassed me about: all Thy billows and Thy waves passed over me.

Then I said, I am cast out of Thy sight: yet I will look again toward Thy holy temple.

The waters compassed me about, even to my soul: the depth closed me round about, the weeds were wrapped about my head.

I went down to the bottoms of the mountains, the earth with her bars was about me forever: yet hast Thou brought up my life from corruption, O Lord my God.

When my soul fainted within me, I remembered the Lord: and my prayer came in unto Thee, into Thine holy temple.

They that observe lying vanities: forsake their own mercy.

But I will sacrifice unto Thee with the voice of thanksgiving

OFFICE FOR PRIME, OR FIRST HOUR.

I will pay that that I have vowed.

Glory be to the Father, &c.

¶ *Then shall the office proceed as follows:*

℣. The Lord be with you.

℟. And with thy spirit.

Let us pray.

Lord, have mercy upon us.
Christ, have mercy upon us.
Lord, have mercy upon us.
Our Father, &c.

¶ *Then shall the Reader say:*

Let us humbly confess our sins to Almighty God.

The Confession: to be made secretly, by each, in a very low voice, so as scarcely to be heard through the Chapel.

ALMIGHTY and most merciful God, Father, Son, and Holy Ghost, I confess to Thee all my sins that I have committed from my childhood even until now; whether knowingly or ignorantly, by day or by night, either sleeping or waking, in word or in deed, in thought or in neglect, through the assaults of the devil or the frailty of my flesh, against Thy Divine will. I implore pardon with all my heart, beseeching Thee that Thy wrath may not come upon me, but that Thy grace may rest upon me now and forevermore. And I beseech Thee, O heavenly Father, O merciful Saviour, O blessed Spirit the Comforter, to have mercy upon me, a sinner, and to bring me safe to everlasting life.

¶ *If a Priest be present, he shall arise and say:*

Almighty God have mercy upon you, and forgive you all your sins, deliver you from all evil, preserve and strengthen you in all goodness, and bring you to everlasting life, through Jesus Christ our Lord.

℟. Amen.

℣. Wilt Thou not turn again and quicken us, O Lord?

℟. That Thy people may rejoice in Thee.

℣. Show us Thy mercy, O Lord.

℟. And grant us Thy salvation.

℣. O Christ, Son of the living God:

℟. Have mercy upon us.

℣. Thou that sittest at the Right Hand of the Father:

℟. Have mercy upon us.

℣. Turn Thee again, O Lord, at the last.

℟. And be gracious unto Thy servants.

℣. Lord, hear our prayer.

℟. And let our cry come unto Thee.

Let us pray.

¶ *Then shall be said the Collect for the day, and after that may be said any other collects or prayers; to which may be added the following final devotions; or the final devotions may immediately follow the Collect for the day.*

O LORD, Heavenly Father, Almighty everliving God, who hast brought us through the darkness of night to the light of the morning, and who, by the light of Thy Word and Holy Spirit dost illumine the darkness of ignorance and sin: we beseech Thee of Thy loving-

OFFICE FOR PRIME, OR FIRST HOUR.

kindness to pour Thy holy light into our souls, that we may ever be devoted to Thee, by whose wisdom we were created, by whose mercy we were redeemed, and by whose providence we are governed, through Jesus Christ our Lord. *Amen.*

O God, the God of spirits and of all flesh with whom no one can compare, whom no one can approach but through Thy beloved Son, that givest the sun to rule the day, the moon and stars to govern the night: vouchsafe to receive our morning sacrifice of prayer and praise, and bless us with Thy spiritual benediction. Keep us this day in Thy fear and love; preserve us in holiness and righteousness, and bring us at length unto everlasting life, through Jesus Christ Thy Son, with whom unto Thee be glory and adoration in the Holy Spirit, now and for ever, world without end. *Amen.*

Glory be to Thee, O Lord, Glory be to Thee.

That this and every day we may pass in the perfecting of holiness, in peace, health, and innocence:

℟. Grant us, O Lord.

That the Angel of peace, our faithful guide, the guardian of our souls and bodies, may encamp round about us, and continually suggest what is needful for our salvation:

℟. Grant us, O Lord.

The pardon and remission of our sins, and strength to withstand every temptation:

℟. Grant us, O Lord.

That we may accomplish the remainder of our life in penitence and godly fear, in favor with Thee, and in charity with all the world:

℟. Grant us, O Lord.

Whatsoever things are true, whatsoever things are honest, whatsoever things are just, whatsoever things are pure, whatsoever things are lovely, whatsoever things are of good report, if there be any virtue and if there be any praise, that we may think on these things and do them:

℟. Grant us, O Lord.

A Christian end of life, without sin, without shame, and, should it please Thee, without pain, and a good answer at the dreadful and fearful judgment-seat of Jesus Christ our Lord:

℟. Grant us, O Lord.

Into the hands of Thy infinite mercy, O Lord, we commend our souls and bodies, our senses, our words, our counsels, our thoughts, our works, and all our actions, with all the necessities of body and soul, our going out and our coming in; our life, our death, and resurrection with Thy saints and elect. *Amen.*

℣. The Lord be with you.

℟. And with thy spirit.

V. Bless we the Lord.

℟. Thanks be to God.

The Grace of the Lord Jesus Christ, and the love of God, and the communion of the Holy Ghost be with you all. *Amen.*

III.

OFFICE FOR THE THIRD HOUR.

9 O'clock, A. M.

IN the Name of the Father, &c.
Our Father, &c.
℣. O Thou who at the Third Hour didst send the Holy Ghost upon Thy Apostles.
℟. Take not away that same Spirit from us, but renew Him daily in our hearts and save us.
℣. O God, make speed, &c.
℟. O Lord, make haste, &c.
℣. Glory be to the Father, &c.
℟. As it was, &c.

HYMN. *Nunc sancte nobis.*

I.

COME Holy Ghost, who ever One,
Art with the Father and the Son,
Shed forth Thy grace within our breast,
And dwell with us a ready guest.

II.

By every power, by heart and tongue,
By act and deed Thy praise be sung;
Inflame with perfect love each sense,
That other's souls may kindle thence.

III.

O Father, that we ask be done,
Through Jesus Christ Thine Only Son,
Who with the Holy Ghost and Thee,
Shall live and reign eternally.
Amen.

¶ *The Psalms, as follows.*
From Advent to Septuagesima.
PSALM XX. *Exaudiat te Dominus.*

THE LORD hear thee in the day of trouble; the Name of the God of Jacob defend thee:
2 Send thee help from the Sanctuary, and strengthen thee out of Sion:
3 Remember all thy offerings, and accept thy burnt-sacrifice:
4 Grant thee thy heart's desire, and fulfil all thy mind.
5 We will rejoice in thy salvation, and triumph in the Name of the Lord our God: the Lord perform all thy petitions.
6 Now know I that the Lord helpeth his Anointed, and will hear him from his holy heaven, even with the wholesome strength of his right hand.
7 Some put their trust in chariots, and some in horses; but we will remember the Name of the Lord our God.
8 They are brought down and fallen; but we are risen and stand upright.

OFFICE FOR THE THIRD HOUR.

9 Save, Lord; and hear us, O King of heaven, when we call upon thee.

From Septuagesima to Easter.

PSALM vi. *Domine, ne in furore.*

O LORD, rebuke me not in thine indignation, neither chasten me in thy displeasure.

2 Have mercy upon me, O Lord, for I am weak: O Lord, heal me, for my bones are vexed.

3 My soul also is sore troubled: but, Lord, how long wilt thou punish me?

4 Turn thee, O Lord, and deliver my soul; O save me, for thy mercies' sake:

5 For in death no man remembereth thee, and who will give thee thanks in the pit?

6 I am weary of my groaning: every night wash I my bed, and water my couch with my tears.

7 My beauty is gone for very trouble, and worn away because of all mine enemies.

8 Away from me, all ye that work vanity; for the Lord hath heard the voice of my weeping.

9 The Lord hath heard my petition; the Lord will receive my prayer.

10 All mine enemies shall be confounded, and sore vexed; they shall be turned back, and put to shame suddenly.

From Easter to Trinity Monday.

PSALM xxvi. *Judica me, Domine.*

BE thou my judge, O Lord, for I have walked innocently: my trust hath been also in the Lord, therefore shall I not fall.

2 Examine me, O Lord, and prove me; try out my reins and my heart.

3 For thy loving-kindness is ever before mine eyes; and I will walk in thy truth.

4 I have not dwelt with vain persons; neither will I have fellowship with the deceitful.

5 I have hated the congregation of the wicked; and will not sit among the ungodly.

6 I will wash my hands in innocency, O Lord; and so will I go to thine altar.

7 That I may show the voice of thanksgiving, and tell of all thy wondrous works.

8 Lord, I have loved the habitation of thy house, and the place where thine honor dwelleth.

9 O shut not up my soul with the sinners, nor my life with the bloodthirsty;

10 In whose hands is wickedness, and their right hand is full of gifts.

11. But as for me, I will walk innocently: O deliver me, and be merciful unto me.

12 My foot standeth right: I will praise the Lord in the congregations.

From Trinity Monday to Advent.

PSALM cxix. 38–48.

Legem pone.

TEACH me, O Lord, the way of thy statutes, and I shall keep it unto the end.

2 Give me understanding, and I shall keep thy law; yea, I shall keep it with my whole heart.

3 Make me to go in the path of thy commandments; for therein is my desire.

4 Incline mine heart unto thy

OFFICE FOR THE THIRD HOUR.

testimonies, and not to covetousness.

5 O turn away mine eyes, lest they behold vanity; and quicken thou me in thy way.

6 O stablish thy Word in thy servant, that I may fear thee.

7 Take away the rebuke that I am afraid of; for thy judgments are good.

8 Behold, my delight is in thy commandments; O quicken me in thy righteousness.

Et veniat super me.

LET thy loving mercy come also unto me, O Lord, even thy salvation, according unto thy Word.

2 So shall I make answer unto my blasphemers; for my trust is in thy Word.

3 O take not the word of thy truth utterly out of my mouth; for my hope is in thy judgments.

4 So shall I alway keep thy law; yea, for ever and ever.

5 And I will walk at liberty; for I seek thy commandments.

6 I will speak of thy testimonies also, even before kings, and will not be ashamed.

7 And my delight shall be in thy commandments, which I have loved.

8 My hands also will I lift up unto thy commandments, which I have loved; and my study shall be in thy statutes.

¶ *The Office shall then be continued as follows.*

[*On Sundays and Feast Days.*

Antiphon. To Father, Son, and Holy Ghost,
The God whom we adore,
Be glory as it was, is now,
And shall be evermore.

The Chapter. Acts ii. 17.

And it shall come to pass in the last days, saith God, I will pour out of My Spirit upon all flesh.

℣. But Thou, O Lord, have mercy upon us.

℟. Thanks be to God.

℣. Incline my heart, O God, to Thy testimonies.

℟. And not to covetousness.

℣. Turn away mine eyes lest they behold vanity.

℟. And quicken Thou me in Thy way.

Let us pray.

WE beseech Thee, O Lord, that the Comforter who proceedeth from Thee may enlighten our minds, and according to Thy Son's promise, lead us into all truth, through Jesus Christ our Lord, who with Thee liveth and reigneth in the unity of the same Holy Spirit world without end. *Amen.*

[*On Week Days.*

Antiphon. O let Thy loving mercies come unto me that I may live.

The Chapter. St. John xiv.

But the Comforter, which is the Holy Ghost, whom the Father will send in My Name, He shall teach you all things, and bring all things to your remembrance, whatsoever I have said unto you. Peace I leave with you, My peace I give unto you; not as the world giveth, give I unto you.

But Thou, O Lord, have mercy upon us.

℟. Thanks be to God.

OFFICE FOR THE THIRD HOUR.

¶ *Then shall the Reader add and say:*

At the third hour He was clothed with a purple robe in mockery; His Head was pierced with the thorny crown; He carried the Cross on His shoulder to the Hill of Calvary; and they crucified Him.

℣. We adore Thee, O Christ, and give thanks to Thee.

℟. For by Thy Holy Cross Thou hast redeemed the world.

Prayers.

O Lord Jesu Christ, Son of the living God, who at the third hour of the day wast led to suffer the death of the cross for the salvation of the world, we humbly pray Thee that by Thy Cross and Passion Thou wouldest graciously blot out all our sins, and mercifully bring us to the glory of Thy kingdom, who livest and reignest God, world without end. *Amen.*

O Lord Jesu Christ, Thou Son of God, Thou Word of the Father that enlightenest every man that cometh into the world, have mercy upon us, and lighten our souls with Thy free Spirit; the Spirit that giveth life; the Spirit of wisdom and forgiveness; the Spirit of holiness and of righteousness; the Spirit of power that is able to overcome all temptations of the devil.

O heavenly King, Thou Comforter and Spirit of truth, who art in every place, and who fillest the whole world with the treasures of Thy goodness, and who givest life, deign to come into our hearts and abide there, and cleanse us from all impurity, O Thou good Spirit, and save our souls alive. *Amen.*

O Saviour, as Thou didst come to Thy disciples, to give them Thy peace, abide with us; breathe Thy life into us, and save us for Thy mercy's sake. *Amen.*

For Lent.

O Thou who wert falsely apprehended and betrayed, deliver us from the false apprehensions and treacheries of men, and grant that we may never withdraw ourselves from Thee; but learn by Thy example to do good with cheerfulness and to suffer evil with patience.

Have mercy upon us, O Lord Jesu, and grant that for Thy sake, who wert stript, mocked, spit upon, wounded and derided for us, we may patiently bear the loss of all things and the derision of all men for Thee.

O Lord, who didst breathe Thy Holy Spirit upon Thy disciples, and didst send Him upon Thy holy Apostles assembled at the third hour; take Him not away from us, Good Lord, but send Him afresh unto us, and make us to know wisdom inwardly. *Amen.*

¶ *Instead of the foregoing prayers may be used any collects or acts of devotion, or special intercessions or litanies.*

℣. The Lord be with you.
℟. And with Thy Spirit.
℣. Bless we the Lord.
℟. Thanks be to God.

The Lord be our keeper; the Lord be our defence on our right hand; the Lord preserve us from all evil and set a watch over our souls; the Lord preserve our going out and our coming in from this time forth forevermore. *Amen.*

IV.

OFFICE FOR THE SIXTH HOUR.

12 O'clock.

IN the Name of the Father, &c.

Our Father, &c.

℣. O Thou, who at the sixth hour didst nail the sins of the world to Thy Cross:

℞. Blot out the handwriting of our offences that is against us and save us.

℣. O God, make speed, &c.

℞. O Lord, make haste, &c.

℣. Glory be to the Father, &c.

℞. As it was in the beginning, &c.

Hymn.

Rector potens, verax Deus.

I.

O GOD of truth, O Lord of might,
That orderest time and change aright,
And send'st the early morning ray,
And light'st the glow of perfect day, —

II.

Extinguish Thou each sinful fire,
And banish every ill desire,
And while Thou keep'st the body whole,
Shed forth Thy peace upon the soul.

III.

O Father, that we ask be done,
Through Jesus Christ Thine Only Son,
Who, with the Holy Ghost and Thee,
Shall live and reign eternally. Amen.

¶ *The Psalms as follows:*

From Advent to Septuagesima.

PSALM xxi. *Domine, in virtute tua.*

THE King shall rejoice in thy strength, O Lord; exceeding glad shall he be of thy salvation.

2 Thou hast given him his heart's desire, and hast not denied him the request of his lips.

3 For thou shalt prevent him with the blessings of goodness, and shalt set a crown of pure gold upon his head.

4 He asked life of thee, and thou gavest him a long life, even for ever and ever.

5 His honor is great in thy salvation; glory and great worship shalt thou lay upon him.

6 For thou shalt give him everlasting felicity, and make him glad with the joy of thy countenance.

7 And why? because the King putteth his trust in the Lord; and in the mercy of the most Highest, he shall not miscarry.

8 All thine enemies shall feel

OFFICE FOR THE SIXTH HOUR.

thy hand; thy right hand shall find out them that hate thee.

9 Thou shalt make them like a fiery oven in time of thy wrath: the Lord shall destroy them in his displeasure, and the fire shall consume them.

10 Their fruit shalt thou root out of the earth, and their seed from among the children of men.

11 For they intended mischief against thee, and imagined such a device as they are not able to perform;

12 Therefore shalt thou put them to flight, and the strings of thy bow shalt thou make ready against the face of them.

13 Be thou exalted, Lord, in thine own strength; so will we sing and praise thy power.

From Septuagesima to Easter.

PSALM xxxii. *Beati, quorum.*

BLESSED is he whose unrighteousness is forgiven, and whose sin is covered.

2 Blessed is the man unto whom the Lord imputeth no sin, and in whose spirit there is no guile.

3 For whilst I held my tongue, my bones consumed away through my daily complaining.

4 For thy hand is heavy upon me day and night, and my moisture is like the drought in summer.

5 I will acknowledge my sin unto thee; and mine unrighteousness have I not hid.

6 I said, I will confess my sins unto the Lord; and so thou forgavest the wickedness of my sin.

7 For this shall every one that is godly make his prayer unto thee, in a time when thou mayest be found; but in the great water floods they shall not come nigh him.

8 Thou art a place to hide me in; thou shalt preserve me from trouble; thou shalt compass me about with songs of deliverance.

9 I will inform thee, and teach thee in the way wherein thou shalt go; and I will guide thee with mine eye.

10 Be ye not like to horse and mule, which have no understanding; whose mouths must be held with bit and bridle, lest they fall upon thee.

11 Great plagues remain for the ungodly; but whoso putteth his trust in the Lord, mercy embraceth him on every side.

12 Be glad, O ye righteous, and rejoice in the Lord; and be joyful, all ye that are true of heart.

From Easter to Trinity Monday.

PSALM cxxxviii. *Confitebor tibi.*

I WILL give thanks unto thee, O Lord, with my whole heart; even before the gods will I sing praise unto thee.

2 I will worship toward thy holy temple, and praise thy name, because of thy lovingkindness and truth; for thou hast magnified thy name and thy word above all things.

3 When I called upon thee, thou heardest me; and enduedst my soul with much strength.

4 All the kings of the earth shall praise thee, O Lord; for they have heard the words of thy mouth.

5 Yea, they shall sing in the ways of the Lord, that great is the glory of the Lord.

OFFICE FOR THE SIXTH HOUR.

6 For though the Lord be high, yet hath he respect unto the lowly; as for the proud, he beholdeth them afar off.

7 Though I walk in the midst of trouble, yet shalt thou refresh me; thou shalt stretch forth thy hand upon the furiousness of mine enemies, and thy right hand shall save me.

8 The Lord shall make good his loving-kindness toward me; yea, thy mercy, O Lord, endureth for ever; despise not then the works of thine own hands.

From Trinity Monday to Advent.

PSALM cxix. 89–104.

In æternum, Domine.

O LORD, thy word endureth for ever in heaven.

2 Thy truth also remaineth from one generation to another; thou hast laid the foundation of the earth, and it abideth.

3 They continue this day according to thine ordinance; for all things serve thee.

4 If my delight had not been in thy law, I should have perished in my trouble.

5 I will never forget thy commandments; for with them thou hast quickened me.

6 I am thine: O save me, for I have sought thy commandments.

7 The ungodly laid wait for me, to destroy me; but I will consider thy testimonies.

8 I see that all things come to an end; but thy commandment is exceeding broad.

Quomodo dilexi!

LORD, what love have I unto thy law! all the day long is my study in it.

2 Thou, through thy commandments, hast made me wiser than mine enemies; for they are ever with me.

3 I have more understanding than my teachers; for thy testimonies are my study.

4 I am wiser than the aged; because I keep thy commandments.

5 I have refrained my feet from every evil way, that I may keep thy word.

6 I have not shrunk from thy judgments; for thou teachest me.

7 O how sweet are thy words unto my throat; yea, sweeter than honey unto my mouth!

8 Through thy commandments I get understanding: therefore I hate all evil ways.

¶ *The Office shall then be continued as follows:*

[*On Sundays and Feast Days.*

Antiphon. To God the Father, Son,
And Spirit ever bless'd,
Eternal Three in One,
All worship be address'd.

The Chapter. 1 St. John v. 7.

There are Three that bear record in Heaven, the Father, the Son, and the Holy Ghost, and these Three are One.

But Thou, O Lord, have mercy upon us.

℟. Thanks be to God.

℣. O Lord, Thy Word endureth forever in heaven.

℟. Thy truth also remaineth from one generation to another.

℣. The Lord is my Shepherd, therefore can I lack nothing.

℟. He shall feed me in a green pasture.

OFFICE FOR THE SIXTH HOUR.

Let us pray.

O LORD, who, as a provident Saviour, dost teach Thy faithful Ones to walk in Thy laws, to search Thy testimonies, and to keep Thy commandments: grant to us, we beseech Thee, Thy righteousness; that we may seek Thee with our whole hearts, understand Thy sayings, tell forth Thy wonders; that we, who have hitherto wandered like lost sheep, restored by Thy kind arms may rejoice in the glories of Paradise, through our Lord Jesus Christ Thy Son, who with Thee liveth and reigneth in the Unity of the Holy Ghost, God blessed for evermore. *Amen.*

[*On Week Days.*

Antiphon. Let me not be disappointed of my hope.

The Chapter. 1 Thess. v. 21-22.

Prove all things; hold fast that which is good; abstain from all appearance of evil.

But Thou, O Lord, have mercy upon us.

℟. Thanks be to God.

¶ *Then shall the Reader add and say.*

At the sixth hour, Jesus hung nailed to the Cross, between two thieves. He was offered vinegar and gall to satiate his tormenting thirst. The Lamb of God was reviled by his enemies.

℣. We adore Thee, O Christ, and give thanks to Thee.

℟. For by Thy Holy Cross Thou hast redeemed the world.

The Prayers.

O Thou, who wast nailed to the Cross on the sixth day on account of the sin of Adam in Paradise, and who wast hanging on the Cross at the sixth hour, blot out the handwriting of our sins, O Jesus our God, and save us.

O Christ our God, Thou didst shed abroad salvation on the earth, when Thou didst stretch Thy Holy Hands upon the Cross.

Therefore do all nations cry aloud unto Thee, O Lord, to Thee belong honor and glory.

O Christ our God, we worship Thee, and beseech Thee to forgive us all our sins.

For Thou didst take up and bear Thy Cross of Thine own will, in order to give life to those whom Thou hadst created, and to save them from the bondage of the enemy.

We cry unto Thee and give thanks unto Thee, for that Thou hast filled us with all joy, O Saviour, since Thou didst come to save the world.

O Lord, Thine is the glory, and the praise, world without end. *Amen.*

O Saviour of the world, who by Thy Cross and precious blood hast redeemed us, save us and help us, we humbly beseech Thee, O Lord.

Have mercy upon us, O Lord, plant in our hearts, we beseech Thee, gentleness and patience, a meek and long-suffering spirit, quietness of mind and stability of soul.

Give us patience in all injuries, and content in all conditions and changes. May we with charity return good for evil. Deliver us from an evil tongue and from an angry contentious spirit. Let

OFFICE FOR THE SIXTH HOUR.

Thy example convert us, Thy gentleness soften us, Thy sufferings and stripes heal us, Thy Blood cleanse us, and Thy death satisfy for and save us.

For Lent.

O LET Thy most precious Blood which issued out of all Thy wounds wash us clean and keep us so. Take us into the embraces of Thine unalterable and everlasting love; for Thou hast opened Thine heart to receive us, let us never be separate from Thee; let Thy patience and love on the Cross reconcile us to all persons and sufferings; let the peace of Thy Cross reconcile us to the Father and bring us peace of conscience; let Thy pains mortify our evil and corrupt affections; let Thy victory give us victory over all our spiritual enemies; let Thy patience satisfy for our impatience, Thy obedience for our disobedience, Thy humility for our pride, Thy love for all our uncharitableness, and make us conformable to Thee.

By Thy loud cries to Thy Father, hear our prayers, and let our cry come unto Thee.

By the vinegar and gall, make all sin bitter to us.

By the commendation of Thy soul into Thy Father's hands, receive our souls into Thy protection here and to Thy everlasting glory hereafter.

By all Thy unknown sufferings,

℟. Have mercy upon us.

By all Thine agonies during the long hours Thou didst hang on the Cross;

℟. Have mercy upon us.

By Thine anguish when forsaken of the Father,

℟. Have mercy upon us.

By the immensity of Thy love, have mercy upon us and fill us with the love of Thee. Be Thou, O Blessed Lord, the supreme object of our love, and the life of our souls.

℟. Amen.

¶ *Instead of the foregoing prayers may be used any Collect, or a Litany.*

℣. The Lord be with you.
℟. And with Thy spirit.
℣. Bless we the Lord.
℟. Thanks be to God.

The peace of our Lord Jesus Christ, the virtue of His sacred Passion, and the power of His Holy Cross, be with us, and between us and all our enemies, now, and in the hour of death. Amen.

V.

OFFICE FOR THE NINTH HOUR.

3 O'clock, P. M.

IN the Name of the Father, &c.

Our Father, &c.

℣. O Thou who at the ninth hour for us sinners and for our sins didst taste death:

℟. Mortify our members which are upon the earth, and whatsoever is contrary to Thy holy will, and save us.

℣. O God, make speed, &c.

℟. O Lord, make haste, &c.

℣. Glory be to the Father, &c.

℟. As it was, &c.

HYMN. *Rerum Deus, tenax vigor.*

I.

O GOD, of all the strength and stay,
Who dost Thyself unmoved abide,
And all the changing hours of day,
In their ordained succession guide.

II.

Thy light upon our evening pour;
So may our life no sunset see,
But death to us an holy door
Of everlasting glory be.

III.

Father of mercies, grant our prayer;

And Thou, coequal, only Son,
Who, with the Spirit Paraclete,
Reign through eternal ages One. *Amen.*

The Psalms as follows.

From Advent to Septuagesima.

PSALM xxvii. *Dominus illuminatio.*

THE LORD is my light and my salvation, whom then shall I fear? the Lord is the strength of my life, of whom then shall I be afraid?

2 When the wicked, even mine enemies and my foes, came upon me to eat up my flesh, they stumbled and fell.

3 Though a host of men were laid against me, yet shall not my heart be afraid; and though there rose up war against me, yet will I put my trust in thee.

4 One thing have I desired of the Lord, which I will require, even that I may dwell in the house of the Lord all the days of my life, to behold the fair beauty of the Lord, and to visit his temple.

5 For in the time of trouble he shall hide me in his tabernacle; yea, in the secret place of his dwelling shall he hide me, and set me up upon a rock of stone.

OFFICE FOR THE NINTH HOUR.

6 And now shall he lift up mine head above mine enemies round about me.

7 Therefore will I offer in his dwelling an oblation, with great gladness: I will sing and speak praises unto the Lord.

8 Hearken unto my voice, O Lord, when I cry unto thee; have mercy upon me, and hear me.

9 My heart hath talked of thee, Seek ye my face: thy face, Lord, will I seek.

10 O hide not thou thy face from me, nor cast thy servant away in displeasure.

11 Thou hast been my succor, leave me not, neither forsake me, O God of my salvation.

12 When my father and my mother forsake me, the Lord taketh me up.

13 Teach me thy way, O Lord, and lead me in the right way, because of mine enemies.

14 Deliver me not over into the will of mine adversaries: for there are false witnesses risen up against me, and such as speak wrong.

15 I should utterly have fainted, but that I believe verily to see the goodness of the Lord in the land of the living.

16 O tarry thou the Lord's leisure; be strong, and he shall comfort thine heart; and put thou thy trust in the Lord.

From Septuagesima to Easter.

PSALM cxliii. *Domine, exaudi.*

HEAR my prayer, O Lord, and consider my desire; hearken unto me for thy truth and righteousness' sake.

2 And enter not into judgment with thy servant; for in thy sight shall no man living be justified.

3 For the enemy hath persecuted my soul; he hath smitten my life down to the ground; he hath laid me in the darkness, as the men that have been long dead.

4 Therefore is my spirit vexed within me, and my heart within me is desolate.

5 Yet do I remember the time past: I muse upon all thy works; yea, I exercise myself in the works of thy hands.

6 I stretch forth my hands unto thee; my soul gaspeth unto thee as a thirsty land.

7 Hear me, O Lord, and that soon; for my spirit waxeth faint: hide not thy face from me, lest I be like unto them that go down into the pit.

8 O let me hear thy lovingkindness betimes in the morning; for in thee is my trust: show thou me the way that I should walk in; for I lift up my soul unto thee.

9 Deliver me, O Lord, from mine enemies; for I flee unto thee to hide me.

10 Teach me to do the thing that pleaseth thee; for thou art my God: let thy loving Spirit lead me forth into the land of righteousness.

11 Quicken me, O Lord, for thy name's sake; and for thy righteousness' sake bring my soul out of trouble.

12 And of thy goodness, slay mine enemies, and destroy all them that vex my soul; for I am thy servant.

OFFICE FOR THE NINTH HOUR.

From Easter to Trinity Monday.
PSALM xlvi. *Deus noster refugium.*

GOD is our hope and strength, a very present help in trouble.

2 Therefore will we not fear, though the earth be moved, and though the hills be carried into the midst of the sea.

3 Though the waters thereof rage and swell, and though the mountains shake at the tempest of the same.

4 The rivers of the flood thereof shall make glad the city of God; the holy place of the tabernacle of the Most Highest.

5 God is in the midst of her, therefore shall she not be removed; God shall help her, and that right early.

6 The heathen make much ado, and the kingdoms are moved; but God hath showed his voice, and the earth shall melt away.

7 The Lord of hosts is with us; the God of Jacob is our refuge.

8 O come hither, and behold the works of the Lord, what destruction he hath brought upon the earth.

9 He maketh wars to cease in all the world; he breaketh the bow, and knappeth the spear in sunder, and burneth the chariots in the fire.

10 Be still then, and know that I am God: I will be exalted among the heathen, and I will be exalted in the earth.

11 The Lord of hosts is with us; the God of Jacob is our refuge.

From Trinity to Advent.
PSALM cxix. 161-176. *Principes persecuti sunt.*

PRINCES have persecuted me without a cause: but my heart standeth in awe of thy word.

2 I am as glad of thy word, as one that findeth great spoils.

3 As for lies, I hate and abhor them; but thy law do I love.

4 Seven times a day do I praise thee; because of thy righteous judgments.

5 Great is the peace that they have who love thy law; and they are not offended at it.

6 Lord, I have looked for thy saving health, and done after thy commandments.

7 My soul hath kept thy testimonies, and loved them exceedingly.

8 I have kept thy commandments and testimonies; for all my ways are before thee.

Appropinquet deprecatio.

LET my complaint come before thee, O Lord; give me understanding according to thy word.

2 Let my supplication come before thee; deliver me according to thy word.

3 My lips shall speak of thy praise, when thou hast taught me thy statutes.

4 Yea, my tongue shall sing of thy word; for all thy commandments are righteous.

5 Let thine hand help me; for I have chosen thy commandments.

6 I have longed for thy saving health, O Lord; and in thy law is my delight.

7 O let my soul live, and it shall praise thee; and thy judgments shall help me.

8 I have gone astray like a sheep that is lost; O seek thy servant, for I do not forget thy commandments.

OFFICE FOR THE NINTH HOUR.

¶ *The Office shall proceed as follows:*

[*On Sundays and Feast Days.*

Antiphon. Of Him and through Him and to Him are all things, to whom be glory for ever and ever. *Amen.*

The Chapter. Eph. iv. 5, 6. Rom. i. 25.

One Lord, one faith, one baptism, one God and Father of all, who is above all and through all and in you all, who is blessed for ever.

But Thou, O Lord, have mercy upon us.

℟. Thanks be to God.

℣. I call with my whole heart; hear me, O Lord.

℟. I will keep Thy statutes.

℣. Cleanse Thou me, O Lord, from my secret faults.

℟. Keep back Thy servant also from presumptuous sins.

Let us pray.

O LORD Jesus Christ, the blessed Son of God, who hast suffered death on the cross for us, that we might thereby be brought to eternal life, have mercy upon us, we beseech Thee, both now, and at the hour of our departure hence; and grant unto us, Thy humble servants, with all good people that have this Thy blessed Passion in devout remembrance, a prosperous and godly life in this present world, and, through Thy grace, eternal glory in the life to come, where with the Father and the Holy Ghost, Thou livest and reignest ever one God, world without end. *Amen.*]

[*On Week Days.*

Antiphon. Give me understanding according to Thy word.

The Chapter. Gal. vi. 2.

Bear ye one another's burdens, and so fulfil the law of Christ.

But Thou, O Lord, have mercy upon us.

℟. Thanks be to God.

¶ *Then shall the Reader say:*

At this hour the Lord Jesus expired, commending His Spirit with a loud cry into the Hands of His Father. The soldier pierced His side with a spear. The earth trembled, and the graves were opened, and many bodies of the Saints which slept arose.

℣. We adore Thee, O Christ, and give thanks to Thee.

℟. For by Thy Holy Cross Thou hast redeemed the world.

The Prayers.

GLORY, honour, and praise be to our Lord Jesus Christ; may all the world adore Thee: blessed be Thy Holy Name, who for us sinners vouchsafedst to be born of a humble Virgin; and blessed be Thine infinite goodness, who diedst on the Cross for our redemption. O Jesus, Son of God and Saviour of mankind, have mercy upon us; and so dispose our lives here by Thy grace, that we may hereafter rejoice with Thee for ever in Thy glory. *Amen.*

SON of God, who didst come down from the bosom of the Father, to save us by taking our

OFFICE FOR THE NINTH HOUR.

nature of the Holy Virgin Mary; by being crucified, and buried, by rising from the dead, and going up on high to the Father; we have sinned against heaven and before Thee; but remember us as Thou didst the penitent thief, when Thou comest into Thy kingdom. *Amen.*

O Lord Jesus Christ, who by Thy death didst take away the sting of death; grant unto us, Thy servants, so to follow in faith where Thou hast led the way, that we may at length fall asleep peacefully in Thee, and awaking up after Thy likeness may be satisfied with it, through Thy mercy who livest and reignest for ever and ever. *Amen.*

Commendation of those in the last Agony.

O GOD, Father of mercies and God of all consolation, who willest not that any that trusteth and hopeth in Thee should perish; we commend into Thy Hands all those Thy servants who must this day depart out of the world, for it is time that Thou have mercy upon them, yea the time is come. Visit them with Thy salvation, and through the Passion and Death of Thine Only Begotten Son, mercifully grant unto them, wheresoever and whosoever they be, pardon and remission of all their sins, and deliverance from their ghostly enemy, that their souls, in this hour of departure, may find Thee a pitying Judge, and washed from all spot in the Blood of Jesus Christ, may pass into Eternal life; through the same Jesus Christ our Lord. *Amen.*

O Christ, who art the true Light, make our spirits worthy to see with joy the light of Thy Glory at that day when Thou callest us home; that we, and all the faithful departed, may rest in hope of Eternal good in the mansions of the righteous until the great day of Thy second coming. *Amen.*

In Lent.

By this Thy death have mercy upon us; kill, crucify, and destroy in us all sin, and let us henceforth live unto Thee.

By that precious water and Blood shed for us have mercy upon us; wash, cleanse, purify, heal our wounded and defiled souls: Then, Blessed Jesus, did the Holy Sacraments flow from Thy sacred Side, the water by which we are regenerated, the Blood by which we are redeemed. Give us evermore the virtue and benefit thereof.

℣. Hide us in Thy pierced side, O Lord.

℟. Until the indignation be overpast.

℣. By Thy prevailing Death, give us life.

℟. And by Thy Resurrection, glory.

Blessed Lord, enclose our souls in Thy pierced Heart, for there we delight to dwell, there to live, and draw life and salvation from Thee. Thy wounded Heart is our sanctuary, our comfort in sorrow, our refuge in trouble; here let us die, and be secure for ever. O, nourish us in Thyself, and we will return all in thanksgiving and love to Thee.

OFFICE FOR THE NINTH HOUR.

¶ *Instead of the foregoing Prayers, may be used a Litany.*

℣. The Lord be with you.
℟. And with thy spirit.
℣. Bless we the Lord.
℟. Thanks be to God.

The Blessing of our Lord Jesus Christ, the virtue of the Holy Spirit, the sign of the Holy Cross, be with us, and defend us, now and in the hour of death. Amen.

VI.

OFFICE FOR VESPERS.

6 O'clock.

IN the Name, &c.
Our Father, &c.
℣. O God, make speed, &c.
℟. O Lord, make haste, &c.
℣. Glory be to the Father, &c.
℟. As it was, &c.
Alleluia.

¶ *But from Septuagesima Sunday to Wednesday in Holy Week inclusive is said instead:*

Praise to Thee, O Lord, we sing,
Of Glory the Eternal King.

¶ *Then shall be said the Psalms, from the Psalter of the Hours.*

¶ *Then shall be said from Epiphany to Septuagesima, and from Trinity Monday to Advent.*

The Chapter. 2 Cor. I. 3, 4.

Blessed be God, even the Father of our Lord Jesus Christ, the Father of mercies and God of all comfort who comforteth us in all our tribulations.
But Thou, O Lord, have mercy upon us.
℟. Thanks be to God.

¶ *At all other times the Chapter shall be taken from the Proper Service of the Season.*

¶ *Then shall be sung this, or some other, hymn —*

HYMN.

I.

ABIDE with me; fast falls
the even-tide;
The darkness deepens; Lord,
with me abide;
When other helpers fail and
comforts flee,
Help of the helpless, O abide
with me.

II.

Swift to its close ebbs out life's
little day;
Earth's joys grow dim, its glories
pass away;
Change and decay in all around
I see,
O Thou who changest not, abide
with me.

III.

I need Thy presence every passing hour;
What but Thy grace can foil the
tempter's power?
Who like Thyself my guide and
stay can be?
Through cloud and sunshine,
Lord, abide with me.

IV.

I fear no foe with Thee at hand
to bless;
Ills have no weight and tears no
bitterness;

OFFICE FOR VESPERS.

Where is death's sting, where, grave, thy victory?
I triumph still if Thou abide with me.

v.

Hold Thou Thy Cross before my closing eyes;
Shine through the gloom and point me to the skies;
Heaven's morning breaks, and earth's vain shadows flee;
In life, in death, O Lord, abide with me.

℣. Let my prayer be set forth.

℟. In Thy sight as the incense.

¶ *Then shall be sung the following Canticle—*
Magnificat.

MY soul doth magnify the Lord: and my spirit hath rejoiced in God my Saviour.

For He hath regarded: the lowliness of His handmaiden.

For behold from henceforth: all generations shall call me blessed.

For He that is mighty hath magnified me: and holy is His Name.

And His mercy is on them that fear him: throughout all generations.

He hath shewed strength with His arm: He hath scattered the proud in the imagination of their hearts.

He hath put down the mighty from their seat: and hath exalted the humble and meek.

He hath filled the hungry with good things: and the rich He hath sent empty away.

He remembering His mercy hath holpen His servant Israel: as He promised to our forefathers, Abraham and his seed for ever.

Glory be to the Father, &c.

¶ *Or this Hymn.*

Joyful Light of the holy glory of the Father,
Immortal, Heavenly, Holy, Blessed,
Jesus Christ;
We, having come to the setting of the sun,
And beholding the evening light,
Praise Father, and Son,
And Holy Spirit, God.
Thee it is meet
At all times to praise,
With reverent voices,
Son of God,
Thou Who givest life;
Wherefore the world glorifieth Thee.

¶ *After the Canticle or Hymn preceding, shall be sung the Antiphon, according to the season, as follows—*

During Advent.

Behold our King cometh, the Lord of the whole earth, and He shall take away the yoke of our captivity.

From Dec. 16, to Dec. 23, the Great Antiphons, on each day one, as marked.

Dec. 16. *O Sapientia.*

O Wisdom, which camest forth out of the mouth of the Most High, and reachest from one end to the other, mightily and sweetly ordering all things: Come and teach us the way of prudence.

Dec. 17. *O Adonai.*

O Lord and Ruler of the House of Israel, who appearedst unto Moses in a flame of fire in

41

OFFICE FOR VESPERS.

the bush, and gavest unto him the law in Sinai: Come and redeem us with an outstretched arm.

Dec. 18. *O Radix Jesse.*

O Root of Jesse, who standest for an Ensign of the people, at whom Kings shall shut their mouths, unto whom the Gentiles shall pray: Come and deliver us, and tarry not.

Dec. 19. *O Clavis David.*

O Key of David and Sceptre of the House of Israel, Thou that openest and no man shutteth, and shuttest and no man openeth: Come and loose the prisoner from the prison-house, and him that sitteth in darkness from the shadow of death.

Dec. 20. *O Oriens.*

O Orient, Brightness of the Eternal Light, and Sun of Righteousness: Come and lighten them that sit in darkness and in the shadow of death.

Dec. 21. *O Rex Gentium.*

O King of the Gentiles and their Desire, the Corner Stone, who madest both one: Come and save man whom Thou hast made out of the dust of the earth.

Dec. 22. *O Emmanuel.*

O Emmanuel, our King and Lawgiver, the Desire of all nations and their Saviour; Come and save us, O Lord our God.

Dec. 23. *O Virgo Virginum.*

O Virgin of Virgins, how shall this be? For neither before thee was any like thee, nor shall there be after. Daughters of Jerusalem, why marvel ye at me? The thing which ye behold is a divine mystery.

Christmas Eve —

Blessed art thou, Mary, that thou hast believed; there shall be performed in thee the things told thee by the Lord. Alleluia.

During Christmas Tide —

The Root of Jesse hath sprung up; the Star hath come out of Jacob: a Virgin hath brought forth the Saviour. We praise Thee, O our God.

During Epiphany Season —

From the East came the Magi into Bethlehem to adore the Lord, and having opened their treasures, precious oblations they offered: Gold, as to a great King; Incense, as to the true God; but Myrrh as for His burial. Alleluia.

From Septuagesima to Lent —

The Lord knoweth how to deliver the godly out of temptations, and to reserve the unjust unto the day of judgment to be punished.

During Lent —

The Bread of God is He that cometh down from heaven and giveth life unto the world.

Easter Tide —

Jesus Himself stood in the midst of them and said: Peace be unto you.

Ascension Day —

O King of Glory, Lord of Hosts, who, triumphant this day, above all heavens hast ascended, abandon us not but send

42

OFFICE FOR VESPERS.

the promise of the Father upon us, the Spirit of truth. Alleluia.

Whitsuntide —

This day are fulfilled the days of Pentecost. Alleluia. This day the Holy Spirit appeared in fire to the disciples, and bestowed on them gifts of graces, sent them into all the world to preach and bear witness; he who hath believed and shall be baptized shall be saved. Alleluia.

On Trinity Sunday only —

Thee, God, the Father unbegotten! Thee, the Son, Only Begotten! Thee, the Spirit, Holy Paraclete! Holy and Undivided Trinity! with our whole heart and mouth we do confess, we do praise, and we do bless; to Thee be glory for evermore.

At all other times the following Antiphon shall be sung —

Come, Holy Ghost, and fill our hearts, inflaming them with Thy love: Thou who gatherest together Thine elect in the Unity of the Faith, descend and rest upon us.

¶ *Then shall follow the Creed and Prayers.*

I believe in God, &c.

℣. The Lord be with you.

℟. And with thy spirit.

Let us pray.

Lord, have mercy upon us.
Christ, have mercy upon us.
Lord, have mercy upon us.
Our Father, &c.

Let us humbly confess our sins to Almighty God.

¶ *The Confession to be made secretly, as at Prime —*

I CONFESS to Almighty God, that I have grievously sinned this day, in thought, word, and deed, through my own fault, through my own most grievous fault. I most earnestly repent of these and all my sins, and am heartily sorry for every thought, word, and deed by which I have displeased the Eyes of Thy Glory and provoked Thy wrath and indignation against me. Wherefore with a penitent and contrite heart, I freely confess the guiltiness of my conscience, and humbly offer these prayers to Thee for pardon, through Jesus Christ.

¶ *If a Priest be present, he shall arise and say:*

Almighty God have mercy upon you, and forgive you all your sins, deliver you from all evil, preserve and strengthen you in all goodness, and bring you to everlasting life, through Jesus Christ our Lord. Amen.

¶ *If no Priest be present, the Reader shall proceed as follows:*

May the great and glorious God of heaven and earth have mercy upon us, forgive us our sins, and bring us to everlasting life. Amen.

May the Almighty hand of our merciful God give us pardon, absolution, and remission of all our sins. Amen.

℣. Abide with us, Lord, for it is toward evening.

℟. And the day is far spent.

℣. Yea, the shadows of the evening are stretched out.

OFFICE FOR VESPERS.

℟. And the day is declining upon us.

℣. Turn Thee again, O Lord, at the last.

℟. And be gracious unto Thy servants.

℣. Let Thy merciful kindness, O Lord, be upon us.

℟. As we do put our trust in Thee.

℣. Let Thy priests be clothed with righteousness.

℟. And Thy saints sing with joyfulness.

℣. O Lord, save the Commonwealth.

℟. And mercifully hear us when we call upon Thee.

℣. O God, save Thy servants and handmaidens.

℟. Which put their trust in Thee.

℣. Give peace in our time, O Lord.

℟. Because there is none other that fighteth for us but only Thou, O God.

℣. Lord, hear our prayer.

℟. And let our cry come unto Thee.

¶ *Then shall be said the Collect for the day, and any other Collects, prayers, or acts of devotion, with or without the final prayers, as follows:*

O GOD who art without beginning and without end, the Maker and Governor of all things through Christ, who hast made the day for works of light, and the night to give rest to our weakness; do Thou now, most kind and gracious Lord, receive this our evening thanksgiving. Thou that hast led us through the length of the day, and hast brought us to the beginning of the night, keep and preserve us by Thy Christ. Grant that we may pass this evening in peace and this night without sin, and finally that we may attain everlasting life through Jesus Christ Thy Son, to whom, with Thee and the Holy Ghost, be glory, honour, and adoration, world without end. *Amen.*

Glory be to the Father of mercies, the Father of men and angels, the Father of our Lord Jesus Christ.

Glory be to the most holy and eternal Son of God, the blessed Saviour and Redeemer of the world, the Advocate of sinners, the Prince of Peace, the Head of the Church, and the mighty Deliverer of all that call on Him.

Glory be to the holy and eternal Spirit of God, the Holy Ghost the Comforter, the Sanctifier of the Elect, and the Giver of life.

All glory and thanks, all honour and power, all love and obedience be to the blessed and undivided Trinity, one God eternal.

All glory and majesty, all praises and dominion be unto Thee, O God, Father, Son, and Holy Ghost, for ever and ever. *Amen.*

¶ *Then may be added the following Benediction.*

The Supreme Majesty of God bless us. ℟. Amen.

The Holy Divinity protect us. ℟. Amen.

The Everlasting Deity keep us. ℟. Amen.

The Glorious Unity comfort us. ℟. Amen.

OFFICE FOR VESPERS.

The Incomprehensible Trinity defend us. ℟. Amen.

The Inestimable Goodness direct us. ℟. Amen.

The Power of the Father guide and govern us. ℟. Amen.

The Wisdom of the Son quicken us. ℟. Amen.

The Virtue of the Holy Ghost enlighten and be with us. ℟. Amen.

The Lord God bless us and defend us from all evil, and bring us to everlasting life. And may the souls of the faithful rest in eternal peace. ℟. Amen.

¶ *Last of all shall be said.*

℣. The Lord be with you.
℟. And with thy spirit.
℣. Bless we the Lord.
℟. Thanks be to God.

Almighty God, Father, Redeemer, Sanctifier, have mercy upon us, and give us peace in this world and in the world to come. Amen.

VII.

OFFICE FOR COMPLINE.

9 O'clock, P. M.

IN the Name, &c.
The Lord Almighty grant us a quiet night and an end of toils.

1 St. Peter v. 8. Brethren, be sober, be vigilant, because your adversary the devil as a roaring lion walketh about seeking whom he may devour: whom resist, steadfast in the faith.

But Thou, O Lord, have mercy upon us.

℞. Thanks be to God.

℣. Our help standeth in the Name of the Lord.

℞. Who hath made heaven and earth.

Our Father, &c.

(*Secretly.*) I confess to God the Father Almighty, to His Only Begotten Son Jesus Christ, and to God the Holy Ghost, and before the whole company of heaven, that I have sinned exceedingly in thought, word, and deed, through my fault, through my own fault, through my own most grievous fault: therefore I pray God to have mercy upon me.

(*The Reader, aloud.*) The Almighty and merciful God grant to us pardon, absolution, and remission of all our sins.

℣. Turn Thou us, O God our Saviour.

℞. And let Thine anger cease from us.

℣. O God, make speed, &c.

℞. O Lord, make haste, &c.

℣. Glory be to the Father, &c.

℞. As it was in the beginning, &c.

¶ *Then shall be said the following Psalms:*

PSALM iv. *Cum invocarem.*

HEAR me, when I call, O God of my righteousness: Thou hast set me at liberty, when I was in trouble; have mercy upon me, and hearken unto my prayer.

2 O ye sons of men, how long will ye blaspheme mine honour, and have such pleasure in vanity, and seek after falsehood?

3 Know this also, that the Lord hath chosen to himself the man that is godly; when I call upon the Lord he will hear me.

4 Stand in awe, and sin not; commune with your own heart, and in your chamber, and be still.

5 Offer the sacrifice of righteousness, and put your trust in the Lord.

6 There be many that say, Who will show us any good?

7 Lord, lift thou up the light of thy countenance upon us.

8 Thou hast put gladness in my heart, since the time that their corn, and wine, and oil increased.

9 I will lay me down in peace, and take my rest; for it is thou Lord only that makest me dwell in safety.

PSALM xxxi. *In te, Domine, speravi.*

IN thee, O Lord, have I put my trust; let me never be put to confusion; deliver me in thy righteousness.

2 Bow down thine ear to me; make haste to deliver me.

3 And be thou my strong rock, and house of defence, that thou mayest save me.

4 For thou art my strong rock, and my castle: be thou also my guide, and lead me for thy Name's sake.

5 Draw me out of the net that they have laid privily for me; for thou art my strength.

6 Into thy hands I commend my spirit; for thou hast redeemed me, O Lord, thou God of truth.

PSALM xci. *Qui habitat.*

WHOSO dwelleth under the defence of the Most High, shall abide under the shadow of the Almighty.

2 I will say unto the Lord, Thou art my hope, and my strong hold; my God, in him will I trust.

3 For he shall deliver thee from the snare of the hunter, and from the noisome pestilence.

4 He shall defend thee under his wings, and thou shalt be safe under his feathers; his faithfulness and truth shall be thy shield and buckler.

5 Thou shalt not be afraid for any terror by night, nor for the arrow that flieth by day;

6 For the pestilence that walketh in darkness, nor for the sickness that destroyeth in the noon-day.

7 A thousand shall fall beside thee, and ten thousand at thy right hand; but it shall not come nigh thee.

8 Yea, with thine eyes shalt thou behold, and see the reward of the ungodly.

9 For thou, Lord, art my hope; thou hast set thine house of defence very high.

10 There shall no evil happen unto thee, neither shall any plague come nigh thy dwelling.

11 For he shall give his angels charge over thee, to keep thee in all thy ways.

12 They shall bear thee in their hands, that thou hurt not thy foot against a stone.

13 Thou shalt go upon the lion and adder: the young lion and the dragon shalt thou tread under thy feet.

14 Because he hath set his love upon me, therefore will I deliver him; I will set him up, because he hath known my name.

15 He shall call upon me, and I will hear him; yea, I am with him in trouble; I will deliver him, and bring him to honour.

16 With long life will I satisfy him, and show him my salvation.

PSALM cxxxiv. *Ecce nunc.*

BEHOLD now, praise the Lord, all ye servants of the Lord;

OFFICE FOR COMPLINE.

2 Ye that by night stand in the house of the Lord, even in the courts of the house of our God.

3 Lift up your hands in the sanctuary, and praise the Lord.

4 The Lord, that made heaven and earth, give thee blessing out of Sion.

Antiphon. I will lay me down in peace and take my rest, for it is Thou Lord only that makest me dwell in safety.

HYMN. *Te lucis ante terminum.*

I.

BEFORE the ending of the day,
Creator of the world, we pray
That Thou with wonted love wouldst keep
Thy watch around us while we sleep.

II.

O let no evil dreams be near,
Nor phantoms of the night appear;
Our ghostly enemy restrain,
Lest aught of sin our bodies stain.

III.

Almighty Father, hear our cry,
Through Jesus Christ our Lord most high,
Who, with the Holy Ghost and Thee,
Doth live and reign eternally. Amen.

The Chapter. Jer. xiv.

Thou, O Lord, art in the midst of us, and we are called by Thy Name; leave us not, O Lord our God.

But Thou, O Lord, have mercy upon us.

℟. Thanks be to God.

℣. Into Thy hands, O Lord, I commend my spirit.

℟. For Thou hast redeemed me, O Lord Thou God of truth.

℣. Keep us, O Lord, as the apple of an eye.

℟. Hide us under the shadow of Thy wings.

Antiphon. Save us, O Lord.

Nunc Dimittis.

Lord, now lettest Thou Thy servant depart in peace: according to Thy word.

For mine eyes have seen: Thy salvation.

Which Thou hast prepared: before the face of all people.

To be a light to lighten the Gentiles: and to be the glory of Thy people Israel.

Glory be to the Father, &c.

Antiphon. Save us, O Lord, watching, guard us sleeping, that we may watch with Christ and rest in peace.

Lord, have mercy.
Christ, have mercy.
Lord, have mercy.
Our Father, &c.

℣. Blessed art Thou, O Lord God of our fathers.

℟. And greatly to be praised and glorified forever.

℣. Let us bless the Father and the Son and the Holy Ghost.

℟. Let us praise and exalt Him forever.

℣. Blessed be Thou, O Lord, in the firmament of heaven.

℟. And greatly to be praised and glorified, and highly exalted forever.

℣. The Almighty and Merciful Lord bless and protect us.

℟. Amen.

℣. Vouchsafe, O Lord, ℟. To keep us this night without sin.

℣. O Lord, have mercy upon us.

℟. Have mercy upon us.

℣. O Lord, let Thy mercy lighten upon us.

℟. As our trust is in Thee.

℣. Lord, hear our prayer.

℟. And let our cry come unto Thee.

Let us pray.

Visit, we beseech Thee, O Lord, this habitation, and drive far from it all snares of the enemy. Let Thy holy angels abide in it to preserve us in peace, and let Thy blessing be ever upon us, through Jesus Christ our Lord. *Amen.*

(*Here may be added* III., IV., VIII., XI., XII. *See pages* 184–6.)

℣. The Lord be with you.

℟. And with thy spirit.

℣. Bless we the Lord.

℟. Thanks be to God.

The Almighty and Merciful Lord, the Father, and the Son, and the Holy Ghost, bless and preserve us now and forevermore. *Amen.*

Here end the Offices of the Seven Hours.

II.

THE PROPER SERVICE OF THE SEASON.

¶ *The Chapters, Hymns, and Responses for the Sunday are to be used throughout its week, and those for a High Feast Day through its Octave.*

First Sunday in Advent.

AT MATINS.

The Chapter. S. Mark i. 1–8.

THE beginning of the Gospel of Jesus Christ the Son of God; as it is written in the prophets, Behold, I send my messenger before thy face which shall prepare thy way before thee. The voice of one crying in the wilderness, Prepare ye the way of the Lord, make his paths straight.

But thou, O Lord, have mercy upon us.

℟. Thanks be to God.

THE HYMN. *Vox clara ecce intonat.*

I.

LO! now a thrilling voice sounds forth,
And chides the darkened shades of earth:
Away, pale dreams, dim shadows fly,
Christ in his might doth shine on high.

II.

Now let the sluggard soul arise,
Which stained by sin and wounded lies:
All ill and harm dispelling far,
Rises the new-born Morning Star.

III.

The Lamb of God is sent below,
Himself to pay the debt we owe;
Oh! for this gift let every voice
With heartfelt songs and tears rejoice.

IV.

That when again His light shines clear,
And wraps the world in sudden fear,
His utmost wrath He may not wreak,
But shield us for His mercy's sake.

V.

To him who comes the world to free,
To God the Son all glory be,
To God the Father as is meet,
To God the Holy Paraclete.
Amen.

℣. The voice of him that crieth in the wilderness. ℟. Prepare ye the way of the Lord; make straight in the desert a highway for our God.

AT VESPERS.

The Chapter. Isaiah ii. 2.

AND it shall come to pass in the last days, that the mountain of the Lord's house shall be established in the top

SECOND SUNDAY IN ADVENT.

of the mountains, and shall be exalted above the hills; and all nations shall flow unto it. And many people shall go and say, Come ye, and let us go up to the mountain of the Lord, to the house of the God of Jacob; and he will teach us of his ways, and we will walk in his paths: for out of Zion shall go forth the law, and the word of the Lord from Jerusalem. And he shall judge among the nations, and shall rebuke many people: and they shall beat their swords into ploughshares, and their spears into pruning-hooks: nation shall not lift up sword against nation, neither shall they learn war any more. O house of Jacob, come ye, and let us walk in the light of the Lord.

R̸. Thou shalt arise, O Lord, and have mercy upon Zion.

V̸. For it is time that thou have mercy upon her, yea the time is come.

R̸. O house of Jacob, come ye, and let us walk in the light of the Lord.

HYMN. *Conditor alme siderum.*

I.

CREATOR of the stars of night,
Thy people's everlasting light,
Jesu, Redeemer, save us all,
And hear thy servants when they call.

II.

Thou cam'st, the Bridegroom of the Bride,
As drew the world to evening tide;
Proceeding from a Virgin shrine,
The spotless Victim all divine.

III.

At whose dread Name, majestic now,
All knees must bend, all hearts must bow;
And things celestial Thee shall own,
And things terrestrial, Lord alone.

IV.

O Thou whose coming is with dread,
To judge and doom the quick and dead,
Preserve us, while we dwell below,
From every insult of the foe.

V.

To Him who comes the world to free,
To God the Son all glory be,
To God the Father as is meet,
To God the Blessed Paraclete.
Amen.

V̸. Drop down, ye heavens, from above.

R̸. And let the skies pour down Righteousness; let the earth open, and let them bring forth salvation.

Second Sunday in Advent.

AT MATINS.

The Chapter. Isaiah lxv. 17, 18.

BEHOLD, I create new heavens and a new earth: and the former shall not be remembered, nor come into mind. But be ye glad and rejoice forever in that which I create: for be-

THIRD SUNDAY IN ADVENT.

hold, I create Jerusalem a rejoicing, and her people a joy.

But thou, O Lord, have mercy upon us.

℟. Thanks be to God.

The Hymn as before.

AT VESPERS.

The Chapter. Isaiah xvi. 1–5.

SEND ye the lamb to the ruler of the land, from Sela to the wilderness, unto the mount of the daughter of Zion. And in mercy shall the throne be established; and he shall sit upon it in truth, in the tabernacle of David, judging, and seeking judgment and hasting righteousness.

℟. The Lord shall teach us his ways and we will walk in his paths.

℣. For the law shall go forth of Zion, and the word of the Lord from Jerusalem.

℟. And we will walk in his paths.

℣. Glory be to the Father, and to the Son, and to the Holy Ghost.

℟. The Lord shall teach us his ways, and we will walk in his paths.

The Hymn as before.

Third Sunday in Advent.

AT MATINS.

The Chapter. Isaiah lv. 6.

SEEK ye the Lord while he may be found, call ye upon him while he is near. Let the wicked forsake his way, and the unrighteous man his thoughts: and let him return unto the Lord, and he will have mercy upon him, and to our God, for he will abundantly pardon.

But thou, O Lord, have mercy upon us.

℟. Thanks be to God.

AT VESPERS.

The Chapter. Isaiah xl. 1.

COMFORT ye, comfort ye, my people, saith your God. Speak ye comfortably to Jerusalem and cry unto her, that her warfare is accomplished, that her iniquity is pardoned; for she hath received of the Lord's hand double for all her sins. The voice of him that crieth in the wilderness, Prepare ye the way of the Lord, make straight in the desert a highway for our God. Every valley shall be exalted, and every mountain and hill shall be made low: and the crooked shall be made straight and the rough places plain: and the glory of the Lord shall be revealed, and all flesh shall see it together: for the mouth of the Lord hath spoken it. ℟. He that shall come, will come, and will not tarry. Now shall there be no more fear in thy borders. ℣. With my soul have I desired thee in the night. ℟. Yea, with my spirit within me will I seek thee early. ℣. Glory be to the Father, and to the Son, and to the Holy Ghost. ℟. He that shall come, will come, and will not tarry.

FROM CHRISTMAS-DAY TO EPIPHANY.

Fourth Sunday in Advent.

AT MATINS.

The Chapter. Zech. xiv. 7, 8, 9.

IT shall come to pass that at evening time it shall be light. And it shall be in that day, that living waters shall go out from Jerusalem; in summer and in winter shall it be. And the Lord shall be king over all the earth.

But thou, O Lord, have mercy upon us.

℟. Thanks be to God.

AT VESPERS.

The Chapter. S. James v. 7, 8.

BE patient, therefore, brethren, unto the coming of the Lord. Behold, the husbandman waiteth for the precious fruit of the earth and hath long patience for it, until he receive the early and latter rain. Be ye also patient; stablish your hearts: for the coming of the Lord draweth nigh.

℟. The Lord is nigh unto all them that call upon him; unto all that call upon him faithfully.

℣. My mouth shall speak the praise of the Lord.

℟. And let all flesh give thanks unto his holy Name for ever and ever.

℣. Come, O Lord, tarry not.

℟. And do away the offences of thy people Israel.

From Christmas-Day to Epiphany.

AT MATINS.

The Chapter. Isaiah lii. 1, 4, 7, 8, 9.

AWAKE, awake; put on thy strength, O Zion; put on thy beautiful garments, O Jerusalem, the holy city: for henceforth there shall no more come into thee the uncircumcised and the unclean. For thus saith the Lord; ye have sold yourselves for nought; and ye shall be redeemed without money. How beautiful upon the mountains are the feet of him that bringeth good tidings, that publisheth peace; that bringeth good tidings of good, that publisheth salvation; that saith unto Zion, Thy God reigneth! Thy watchmen shall lift up the voice. with the voice together shall they sing: for they shall see eye to eye, when the Lord shall bring again Zion. Break forth into joy, sing together, ye waste places of Jerusalem: for the Lord hath comforted his people, he hath redeemed Jerusalem.

But Thou, O Lord, have mercy upon us. ℟. Thanks be to God.

HYMN. *Adeste Fideles.*

I.

O COME all ye Faithful, joyful and triumphant,
O come ye, O come ye to Bethlehem!
Born here behold Him, Lord and king of angels!
　O come and let us worship,
　O come and let us worship,
O come and let us worship, adoring the Lord!

FROM CHRISTMAS-DAY TO EPIPHANY.

II.

God out of Godhead! Light from Light Eternal!
Lo, in the Virgin Womb His chosen shrine!
God over all, begotten not created!
 O come and let us worship,
 O come and let us worship,
O come and let us worship, adoring the Lord!

III.

Sing, Alleluia! ye choral host of Angels!
Sing, O Celestial Court on high!
Glory to God! All glory in the highest!
 O come and let us worship,
 O come and let us worship,
O come and let us worship, adoring the Lord!

IV.

Thou who wast born this holy day of Mary,
 O Jesu, to Thee be blessing, glory, and praise!
Word of th' Eternal Father, now Incarnate!
 O come and let us worship,
 O come and let us worship,
O come and let us worship, adoring the Lord!

℣. Blessed is He that cometh in the Name of the Lord.

℟. God is the Lord, who hath showed us light.

AT VESPERS.

The Chapter. Heb. i. 1, 2.

GOD, who at sundry times and in divers manners spake unto the fathers by the prophets, hath in these last days spoken unto us by His Son.

℟. God is the Lord, who hath showed us light.

℣. The Word was made Flesh. Alleluia.

℟. And dwelt among us. Alleluia.

℣. Glory be to the Father, and to the Son, and to the Holy Ghost.

℟. The Word was made Flesh and dwelt among us. Alleluia.

THE HYMN. *Veni Redemptor Gentium.*

I.

COME, Redeemer of the nations;
Thou the Virgin's mystic birth,
Wonder of all generations,
God most meekly born on earth.

II.

Not in carnal union given;
By the Spirit's mystery,
Flesh is made the Word from Heaven,
And the promised seed draws nigh.

III.

God is Man, in way most holy,
Pure from every stain abhorred;
And the Virgin's breast all lowly
Is the temple of the Lord.

IV.

From the Father's glory bending,
He again with Him shall stand;
And to Hell in death descending,
Rise in life to God's right hand.

V.

Brightly gleams Thy holy manger,
And new glories gild the night,
Darkness now to us a stranger,
We shall dwell in fadeless light.

VI.

Glory to our God be given,
To the Son and Paraclete;

THE FEAST OF THE EPIPHANY ONLY.

Worshipped evermore in Heaven,
With due praise and honour meet. Amen.

℣. As a bridegroom out of his chamber:
℟. The Lord cometh forth to run his course.

The Feast of the Epiphany only.

AT MATINS.

The Chapter. Isaiah lx. 1.

ARISE, shine, for thy light is come, and the glory of the Lord is risen upon thee.
But Thou, O Lord, have mercy upon us. ℟. Thanks be to God.

THE HYMN. *Jesus refulsit omnium.*

I.

JESUS hath shone benignly forth,
Redeemer of the tribes of Earth;
Let all the faithful far and near,
The praises of His deeds declare.

II.

Whose birth the Star's bright rays revealed,
Resplendent in the ethereal field;
The Magi guiding in the way,
To Him who in the manger lay.

III.

Prostrate the Infant they adore,
With linen meanly swathed o'er,
Confess Him Very God, and bring
Their mystic offerings to their King.

IV.

On us in mercy here below,
Thy help and comfort e'er bestow,
And rapt from Satan's drear domain,
With Thee above the stars to reign.

℣.

All glory, Lord, to Thee we pay,
For Thine Epiphany to-day;
All glory as is ever meet,
To Father and to Paraclete.
Amen.

℣. It is the Lord that commandeth the waters; it is the glorious God that maketh the thunder.

℟. The Voice of the Lord is mighty in operation: the Voice of the Lord is a glorious Voice.

AT VESPERS.

The Chapter. Isaiah lx. 2, 3

THE Lord shall arise upon thee, O Jerusalem, and His glory shall be seen upon thee. And the Gentiles shall come to thy light, and Kings to the brightness of thy rising.

℟. The Kings of Tharsis and of the Isles shall give presents. Alleluia, Alleluia.

℣. The Kings of Arabia and Saba shall bring gifts.

℟. Alleluia, Alleluia.

℣. Glory be to the Father, and to the Son, and to the Holy Ghost.

℟. The Kings of Tharsis and of the Isles shall give presents. Alleluia, Alleluia.

℣. All kings shall fall down before Him.

℟. All nations shall do Him service.

FROM SEPTUAGESIMA TO ASH WEDNESDAY.

The Hymn. *Hostis Herodes impie.*

I.

WHY, impious Herod, vainly fear,
That Christ the Saviour cometh here?
He takes not earthly realms away,
Who gives the crown that lasts for aye.

II.

To greet His birth the wise men went,
Led by the star before them sent;
Called on by light, towards Light they press'd,
And by their gifts, their God confess'd.

III.

In holy Jordan's purest wave,
The heavenly Lamb vouchsaf'd to lave;
That He to whom was sin unknown,
Might cleanse His People from their own.

IV.

New miracle of Power divine,
The water reddens into wine:
He spake the word, and pour'd the ways
In other streams than Nature gave.

V.

All glory, Lord, to Thee we pay,
For Thine Epiphany to-day:
All glory as is ever meet,
To Father and to Paraclete.
Amen.

℣. All they from Sheba shall come.

℟. They shall bring gold and incense, and they shall show forth the praises of the Lord.

From Septuagesima to Ash Wednesday.

AT MATINS.

The Chapter. 1 Cor. ix. 24.

KNOW ye not that they which run in a race run all, but one receiveth the prize? So run, that ye may obtain. And every one that striveth for the mastery is temperate in all things. Now they do it to obtain a corruptible crown, but we an incorruptible. I therefore so run, not as uncertainly; so fight I, not as one that beateth the air: But I keep under my body, and bring it into subjection: lest that by any means, when I have preached to others, I myself should be a castaway.

But Thou, O Lord, have mercy upon us. ℟. Thanks be to God.

AT VESPERS.

The Chapter. Jeremiah vi. 16.

THUS saith the Lord, Stand ye in the ways, and see, and ask for the old paths, where is the good way, and walk therein, and ye shall find rest for your souls.

℟. Thanks be to God.

℣. Thou Lord in the beginning hast laid the foundation of the earth.

ASH WEDNESDAY TO FOURTH SUNDAY IN LENT.

℟. And the heavens are the work of Thy hands.

℣. They shall perish, but Thou shalt endure.

℟. And as a vesture shalt Thou change them, and they shall be changed; but Thou art the same, and Thy years shall not fail.

℣. Be merciful unto me, O God, be merciful unto me.

℟. For my soul trusteth in Thee.

The following Hymn is sung at any hour, during the weeks between Septuagesima and Lent.

HYMN. *Alleluia, dulce carmen.*

I.

ALLELUIA, song of sweetness,
Voice of joy that cannot die,
Alleluia is the anthem
Ever dear to choirs on high;
In the house of God abiding,
Thus they sing eternally.

II.

Alleluia thou resoundest
True Jerusalem and free;
Alleluia, joyful Mother,
All thy children sing with thee;
But by Babylon's sad waters,
Mourning Exiles now are we.

III.

Alleluia cannot always
Be our song while here below,
Alleluia our transgressions
Make us for a while forego;
For the solemn time is coming
When our tears for sin must flow.

IV.

Therefore, in our hymns we pray Thee,
Grant us, Blessed Trinity,
At the last to keep Thine Easter
In our home beyond the sky;
There to Thee for ever singing
Alleluia joyfully. Amen.

From Ash Wednesday to the Fourth Sunday in Lent.

AT MATINS.

The Chapter. Joel ii. 12, 13.

TURN ye even unto me, saith the Lord, with all your heart, and with weeping and with fasting and with mourning. And rend your hearts, and not your garments, and turn unto the Lord your God.

But Thou, O Lord, have mercy upon us.

℟. Thanks be to God.

HYMN. *Audi benigne Conditor.*

I.

O MAKER of the world, give ear!
Accept the prayer, and own the tear,
Towards Thy seat of mercy sent,
In this most holy fast of Lent.

II.

Each heart is manifest to Thee,
Thou knowest our infirmity;
Forgive Thou then each soul that fain
Would seek to Thee, and turn again.

III.

Our sins are manifold and sore,
But pardon them that sin deplore;

ASH WEDNESDAY TO FOURTH SUNDAY IN LENT

And, for Thy Name's sake, make each soul
That feels and owns its languor whole.

IV.

So mortify we every sense,
By grace of outward abstinence,
That from each stain and spot of sin,
The soul may keep her fast within.

V.

Grant, O Thou Blessed Trinity,
Grant, O Essential Unity,
That this our fast of forty days
May work our profit and Thy praise. Amen.

℣. His faithfulness and truth shall be thy shield and buckler.

℟. Thou shalt not be afraid for any terror by night.

AT VESPERS.

The Chapter. Rom. xv. 13.

NOW the God of hope fill you with all joy and peace in believing, that ye may abound in hope through the power of the Holy Ghost.

But Thou, O Lord, have mercy upon us.

℟. Thanks be to God.

℣. He shall deliver thee from the snare of the hunter.

℟. And from the noisome pestilence.

℣. He shall defend thee under His wings.

℟. And thou shalt be safe under His feathers.

HYMN. *Jesu quadragenaria.*

I.

JESU! who this our Lenten tide
Of abstinence hast sanctified;
And who to amend our soul's estate
This holy fast didst consecrate.

II.

So unto Paradise once more,
By sober converse to restore,
The souls whom thence enticing lust
Insatiate, had to ruin thrust;

III.

Be with Thy Church in saving power,
In this her penitential hour;
When for the sins of bygone days,
In plenteousness of tears she prays.

IV.

To all our heinous past offence,
Thy gracious pardon, Lord, dispense;
And let Thy mercy guard us still
From crimes that threaten future ill.

V.

So cleansed in spirit in thine eyes,
By this our fasting sacrifice,
May we Thy paschal joys prepare
With meet and reverent love to share.

VI.

O Father, that we ask be done
Through Jesus Christ Thine Only Son;
Who, with the Holy Ghost and Thee,
Shall live and reign eternally. Amen.

℣. He shall give His angels charge over thee.

℟. To keep thee in all thy ways.

Fourth Sunday in Lent to Palm Sunday.

AT MATINS.

The Chapter. St. John viii. 12.

THEN spake Jesus, I am the Light of the World; he that followeth Me shall not walk in darkness, but shall have the light of life.

But Thou, O Lord, have mercy upon us.

℟. Thanks be to God.

HYMN. *Pange lingua gloriosi.*

[*This hymn, if too long, may be begun at the verse, "Thirty years among us dwelling."*]

I.

SING, my tongue, the glorious battle
With completed victory rife;
And above the Cross's trophy
Tell the triumph of the strife;
How the world's Redeemer conquered
By surrendering of His life.

II.

God his Maker, sorely grieving
That the first-made Adam fell,
When he ate the fruit of sorrow,
Whose reward was death and hell,
Noted then this word, the ruin
Of the ancient word to quell.

III.

For the work of our salvation
Needs would have his order so,
And the multiform deceiver's
Art by art would overthrow,
And from thence would bring the med'cine,
Whence the insult of the foe.

IV.

Wherefore, when the sacred fulness
Of th' appointed time was come,
This world's Maker left His Father,
Sent the heavenly mansion from,
And proceeded, God incarnate
Of the Virgin's Holy Womb.

V.

Thirty years among us dwelling
His appointed time fulfill'd,
Born for this, He meets His Passion,
For that this He freely will'd.
On the Cross the Lamb is lifted
Where His lifeblood shall be spill'd.

VI.

He endur'd the nails, the spitting,
Vinegar, and spear, and reed;
From that Holy Body broken
Blood and water forth proceed:
Earth and stars, and sky and ocean,
By that flood from stain are freed.

VII.

Faithful Cross! above all other
One and only noble tree!
None in foliage, none in blossom,
None in fruit Thy peers may be!
Sweetest wood and sweetest iron!
Sweetest weight is hung on Thee.

VIII.

Bend thy boughs, O Tree of Glory!
Thy relaxing sinews bend;
For awhile the ancient rigor
That thy birth bestow'd suspend:
And the King of heavenly beauty
On thy bosom gently tend!

FOURTH SUNDAY IN LENT TO PALM SUNDAY.

IX.

Thou alone wast counted worthy
This world's Ransom to uphold;
For a shipwreck'd race preparing
Harbor, like the Ark of old;
With the sacred Blood anointed
From the smitten Lamb that rolled.

X.

To the Trinity be glory
Everlasting as is meet,
Equal to the Father, equal
To the Son and Paraclete;
Trinal Unity whose praises
All created things repeat.
Amen.

℣. Deliver me from mine enemies, O God.

℟. Defend me from them that rise up against me.

AT VESPERS.

The Chapter. Daniel vi. 26, 27.

HE is the living God and steadfast for ever, and His kingdom that which shall not be destroyed, and His dominion shall be even unto the end. He delivereth and rescueth, and He worketh signs and wonders in heaven and in earth.

But Thou, O Lord, have mercy upon us.

℟. Thanks be to God.

℣. The ungodly compassed me about and afflicted me without a cause.

℟. But Thou, O Lord, art my defender.

℣. For trouble is hard at hand.

℟. And there is none to help me.

℣. Deliver me from mine enemies, O God.

℟. Defend me from them that rise up against me.

HYMN. *Vexilla Regis prodeunt.*

I.

THE Royal Banners forward go;
The Cross shines forth in mystic glow;
Where He in flesh, our flesh who made,
Our sentence bore, our ransom paid.

II.

Where deep for us the spear was dy'd,
Life's torrent rushing from His side,
To wash us in that precious flood
Where mingled water flow'd and Blood.

III.

Fulfill'd is all that David told,
In true prophetic song of old,
Amidst the nations God saith he
Hath reign'd and triumph'd from the Tree.

IV.

O Tree of beauty, Tree of light!
O Tree with royal purple dight!
Elect on whose triumphal breast
Those holy limbs should find their rest:

V.

On whose dear arms, so widely flung,
The weight of this world's ransom hung:
The price of human kind to pay,
And spoil the spoiler of his prey.

FROM MAUNDAY-THURSDAY TO EASTER-DAY.

VI.
To Thee, Eternal Three in one,
Let homage meet by all be done:
Whom by the Cross Thou dost restore.

Preserve and govern evermore. Amen.

℣. They gave me gall to eat.
℟. And when I was thirsty they gave me vinegar to drink.

Palm Sunday.

AT MATINS.

The Chapter. Phil. ii. 10, 11.

AT the Name of Jesus every knee shall bow, of things in heaven and things in earth, and things under the earth; and every tongue shall confess that Jesus Christ is Lord to the glory of God, the Father.

But Thou, O Lord, have mercy upon us.

℟. Thanks be to God.

AT VESPERS.

The Chapter. Hosea vi. 3, 4.

O MY people, what have I done unto thee? And wherein have I wearied thee? Testify against me. For I brought thee up out of the land of Egypt, and redeemed thee out of the house of bondage; and I sent before thee Moses, Aaron, and Miriam.

℟. But Thou hast prepared a Cross for Thy Saviour.

℣. Lift up your heads, O ye gates, and be ye lift up ye everlasting doors.

℟. And the King of Glory shall come in.

℣. Blessed be the King that cometh in the Name of the Lord.

℟. Peace in heaven and glory in the highest.

From Maunday-Thursday to Easter-Day.

¶ *The order for Maunday-Thursday shall be as follows: After the invocation of the Blessed Trinity and the Lord's Prayer, the Psalms shall be at once begun, and sung without Gloria Patri, which shall not be said again until the Matins of Easter Day. Then shall be said immediately Benedictus, without Gloria Patri. Then all kneeling, is said—*

LORD, have mercy upon us.
Christ, have mercy upon us.
Lord, have mercy upon us.

℣. Christ became obedient for us unto death.
℟. Even the death of the Cross.

¶ *Then shall be said one of the following Psalms*: 6, 32, 38, 51, 102, 130, 143.

¶ *And then without "The Lord be with you, &c." is immediately said—*

The Collect.

ALMIGHTY GOD, we beseech thee graciously to behold this Thy family, for which our Lord Jesus Christ

FROM EASTER-DAY TO LOW SUNDAY.

was contented to be betrayed, and given up into the hands of wicked men, and to suffer death upon the Cross, who now liveth and reigneth with Thee and the Holy Ghost, ever one God, world without end. Amen.

¶ *Thus end the Matins.*

¶ *So shall be said all the Hours till Easter Day, except, of course, with their own Psalms.*

¶ *On Good Friday the Collect shall end at the word Cross.*

¶ *On Easter Even, the proper Collect for the Day shall be used, but all else shall be as on the two preceding days.*

From Easter-Day to Low Sunday.

¶ *No Chapter is said: but immediately after the Psalms, is said —*

At Matins, Prime, and Vespers.

℣. THE Lord is risen from the tomb.

℟. Who died to save us from our doom. Alleluia.

At the other Hours, except Compline.

℣. In Thy resurrection, O Christ.

℟. Let heaven and earth rejoice. Alleluia.

¶ *After this, at each Office, shall be said immediately —*

℣. The Lord be with you.

℟. And with Thy Spirit.

Let us pray.

The Collect.

ALMIGHTY GOD, who through Thine only begotten Son Jesus Christ hast overcome death, and opened unto us the gate of everlasting life; We humbly beseech Thee, that, as by Thy special grace preventing us Thou dost put into our minds good desires, so by Thy continual help we may bring the same to good effect, through Jesus Christ our Lord, who liveth and reigneth with Thee and the Holy Ghost, ever one God, world without end. Amen.

℣. Bless we the Lord.

℟. Thanks be to God.

Benediction. Heb. xiii. 20, 21.

20. NOW the God of peace, that brought again from the dead our Lord Jesus, that great Shepherd of the sheep, through the blood of the everlasting covenant, make you perfect in every good work to do his will, working in you that which is well pleasing in his sight, through Jesus Christ; to whom be glory for ever and ever. Amen.

¶ *Thus shall the Hours be said, except Compline, during Easter Week.*

From Low Sunday to Ascension-Day.

AT MATINS.

The Chapter. Rom. vi. 4.

LIKE as Christ was raised up from the dead by the glory of the Father, even so we also should walk in newness of life.

But Thou, O Lord, have mercy upon us.

℟. Thanks be to God.

HYMN. *Sermone blando Angelus.*

I.

WITH gentle voice the Angel gave
The women tidings at the grave;
"Forthwith your Master shall ye see;
He goes before to Galilee."

II.

And while with fear and joy they press'd,
To tell these tidings to the rest,
Their Lord, their living Lord they meet,
And see His form, and kiss His feet.

III.

Th' Eleven, when they hear, with speed
To Galilee forthwith proceed;
That there they may behold once more
The Lord's dear Face, as oft afore.

IV.

In this our bright and paschal day
The sun shines out with purer ray:
When Christ, to earthly sight made plain,
The glad Apostles see again.

V.

The wounds, the riven wounds, He shows
Of that His flesh with light that glows,
In loud accord, both far and nigh,
The Lord's arising testify.

VI.

O Christ, the King, who lov'st to bless,
Do Thou our hearts and souls possess;
To Thee our praise, that we may pay,
To whom all laud is due for aye.

VII.

We pray Thee, King with glory deck'd,
In this our Paschal joy protect,
From all that death would fain effect,
Thy ransom'd flock, Thine own elect.

VIII.

To Thee, who, dead, again dost live,
All glory, Lord, Thy people give;
All glory, as is ever meet,
To Father and to Paraclete. *Amen.*

℣. The Lord hath risen from the tomb.

℟. Who died to save us from our doom. Alleluia.

AT VESPERS.

The Chapter. Acts i. 3.

JESUS also shewed Himself alive, after His Passion, by many infallible proofs, being seen of them forty days, and

FROM ASCENSION-DAY TO WHIT-SUNDAY.

speaking of the things pertaining to the kingdom of God.

℟. Jesu Christ, Son of the living God, have mercy upon us.

℣. In Thy Resurrection, O Christ.

℟. Let heaven and earth rejoice.

℣. I shall not die, but live. Alleluia.

℟. And declare the works of the Lord. Alleluia.

HYMN. *Ad cœnam Agni providi.*

I.

THE Lamb's high banquet we await,
In snow-white robes of royal state:
And now, the Red Sea's channel past,
To Christ, our Prince, we sing at last.

II.

Upon the altar of the Cross,
His Body hath redeem'd our loss.
And tasting of His roseate Blood,
Our life is hid with Him in God.

III.

That Paschal eve God's arm was bar'd;
The devastating angel spar'd:
By strength of hand our hosts went free,
From Pharaoh's ruthless tyranny.

IV.

Now Christ, our Paschal Lamb, is slain,
The Lamb of God that knows no stain,
The true Oblation offer'd here,
Our own unleaven'd bread sincere.

V.

O Thou, from whom Hell's monarch flies,
O great, O very sacrifice!
Thy captive people are set free,
And endless life restored in Thee.

VI.

For Christ, arising from the dead,
From conquer'd hell victorious sped:
And thrust the tyrant down to chains,
And Paradise for man regains.

VII.

To Thee, who, dead, again dost live,
All glory, Lord, thy people give;
All glory, as is ever meet,
To Father and to Paraclete.
Amen.

℣. Abide with us.

℟. For it is toward Evening, and the day is far spent. Alleluia.

From Ascension-Day to Whit-Sunday.

AT MATINS.

The Chapter. Hebrews ix. 24.

FOR Christ is not entered into the holy places made with hands, which are the figures of the true: but into heaven itself, now to appear in the presence of God for us.

But Thou, O Lord, have mercy upon us.

℟. Thanks be to God.

HYMN. *Hymnum canamus gloriæ.*

I.

SING we triumphant hymns of praise,

FROM ASCENSION-DAY TO WHIT-SUNDAY.

New hymns to heaven exulting raise;
Christ, by a road before untrod,
Ascendeth to the Throne of God.

II.

The holy Apostolic band
Upon the Mount of Olives stand,
And with the Virgin Mother see
Jesu's resplendent Majesty.

III.

To whom the Angels, drawing nigh,
"Why stand and gaze upon the sky?
"This is the Saviour," thus they say,
"This is His noble triumph day.

IV.

"Again shall ye behold Him, so,
"As ye to-day have seen Him go,
"In glorious pomp ascending high
"Up to the portals of the sky."

V.

O grant us thitherward to tend,
And with unwearied hearts ascend
Toward thy Kingdom's Throne where Thou,
As is our faith, art seated now.

VI.

Be Thou our Joy, and Thou our Guard,
Who art to be our great Reward;
Our glory and our boast in Thee
For ever and for ever be!

VII.

All glory, Lord, to Thee we pay,
Ascending o'er the stars to-day;
All glory, as is ever meet,
To Father and to Paraclete.
Amen.

℣. God is gone up with a merry noise.
℟. And the Lord with the sound of the trumpet. Alleluia.

AT VESPERS.

The Chapter. Hebrews xii. 1, 2.

LET us run with patience the race that is set before us, looking unto Jesus, the author and finisher of our faith; who for the joy that was set before Him, endured the Cross, despising the shame, and is set down at the right hand of the Throne of God.

℟. Thou art the King of Glory, O Christ.

℣. Thou art gone up on high, Thou hast led captivity captive.

℟. And hast given good gifts to men.

℣. The Lord's seat is in heaven. Alleluia, Alleluia.

℟. His eyes behold the children of men. Alleluia.

℣. I ascend to my Father and your Father.

℟. To my God and your God.

HYMN. *Æterne Rex altissime.*

I.

ETERNAL Monarch, King most high,
Whose Blood hath brought redemption nigh,
By whom the death of Death was wrought,
And conqu'ring grace's battle fought.

II.

Ascending to the Throne of might,
And seated at the Father's right,

FROM WHIT-SUNDAY TO TRINITY SUNDAY.

All power in heaven is Jesu's own,
That here His manhood had not known.

III.

That so, in Nature's triple frame,
Each heavenly and each earthly name,
And things in Hell's abyss abhorr'd,
May bend the knee and own Him Lord.

IV.

Yea, angels tremble when they see
How changed is our humanity,
That flesh hath purg'd what flesh had stain'd,
And God, the Flesh of God, hath reign'd.

V.

Be Thou our joy and Thou our Guard,
Who art to be our great Reward;
Our glory and our boast in Thee
For ever and for ever be!

VI.

All glory, Lord, to Thee we pray,
Ascending o'er the stars to-day;
All glory, as is ever meet,
To Father and to Paraclete.
Amen.

℣. Thou art gone up on high, O Christ.

℟. Thou hast led captivity captive. Alleluia.

From Whit-Sunday to Trinity Sunday.

AT MATINS.

The Chapter. Isaiah lv. 1.

HO, every one that thirsteth, come ye to the waters, and he that hath no money; come ye, buy and eat; yea, come, buy wine and milk without money and without price.

But Thou, O Lord, have mercy upon us.

℟. Thanks be to God.

HYMN. *Veni Creator Spiritus.*

I.

COME, Holy Ghost, our souls inspire,
And lighten with celestial fire:
Thou the anointing Spirit art
That dost thy seven-fold gifts impart.

II.

Thy blessed unction from above
Is comfort, life, and fire of love:
Enable with perpetual light
The dulness of our blinded sight.

III.

Anoint and cheer our soiled face
With the abundance of thy grace:
Keep far our foes, give peace at home:
Where Thou art guide no ill can come.

IV.

Teach us to know the Father, Son,
And Thee of both to be but one;
That through the ages all along,
This may be our endless song.

FROM WHIT-SUNDAY TO TRINITY SUNDAY.

V.
Praise to thy eternal merit,
Father, Son, and Holy Spirit.
Amen.

℣. The Apostles did speak with other tongues.

℟. The wonderful works of God. Alleluia.

AT VESPERS.

The Chapter. Ephes. iii. 16, 17.

THE Lord grant you, according to the riches of his glory, to be strengthened with might by his Spirit in the inner man; that Christ may dwell in your hearts by faith.

℟. Thanks be to God.

℣. And it shall come to pass in the last days, saith God.

℟. That I will pour out my Spirit upon all flesh.

℣. He hath increased his people exceedingly.

℟. And made them stronger than their enemies.

℣. Strengthen the thing that Thou hast wrought in us, O Lord.

℟. For thy temple's sake at Jerusalem.

℣. Let thy loving Spirit lead me forth.

℟. Into the land of righteousness.

HYMN. *Beata nobis gaudia.*

I.

BLEST joys for mighty wonders wrought
The year's revolving orb has brought,
What time the Holy Ghost in flame,
Upon the Lord's disciples came.

II.

The quivering fire their heads bedew'd,
In cloven tongues' similitude,
That eloquent their words might be,
And fervid all their charity.

III.

In varying tongues the Lord they prais'd;
The gathering people stood amaz'd;
And whom the Comforter divine
Inspir'd, they mock'd as full of wine.

IV.

These things were done in type to-day,
When Easter tide had worn away,
The number told which once set free
The captive at the jubilee.

V.

Thy servants, falling on their face,
Beseech thy mercy, God of grace,
To send us, from thy heavenly seat,
The blessings of the Paraclete.

VI.

To God the Father, God the Son,
And God the Spirit, praise be done;
And Christ the Lord upon us pour
The Spirit's gift for evermore.
Amen.

℣. The Spirit of the Lord filleth the world.

℟. And that which containeth all things hath knowledge of the voice. Alleluia.

On Trinity Sunday.

AT MATINS.

The Chapter. Rev. iv. 8.

AND they rest not day and night, saying, Holy, Holy, Holy, Lord God Almighty, which was and is, and is to come.

℟. Let us bless the Father, and the Son, and the Holy Ghost. Alleluia, Alleluia.

℣. Praise Him, and magnify Him for ever.

℟. Alleluia, Alleluia.

℣. Blessed art Thou in the firmament of heaven.

℟. And above all to be praised and glorified for ever. *Amen.*

HYMN. *Ave colenda Trinitas.*

I.

ALL hail! Adorèd Trinity!
All hail! Adorèd Unity!
The Father God, and God the Son,
And God the Spirit, Three in One!

II.

Behold to Thee this blessed day,
Our grateful thanks we duly pay,
For thy rich gifts of priceless worth,
The saving health of all on earth.

III.

Thee, Three in One, we thus adore,
Thee, One in Three, for evermore;
In thy sweet mercy may we find
A shelter sure for all mankind.

IV.

O Trinity! O Unity!
Be with us as we worship thee;
And to the angels' songs in light
Our prayers and praises now unite. *Amen.*

℣. Blessed be the Name of the Lord.

℟. From this time forth for evermore.

AT VESPERS.

The Chapter. Romans xi. 33–36.

O THE depth of the riches both of the wisdom and knowledge of God! How unsearchable are his judgments, and his ways past finding out! For of him, and through him, and to him are all things; to whom be glory for ever. *Amen.*

℟. Thanks be to God.

℣. Blessed be the Name of the Lord.

℟. From this time forth for evermore.

℣. Thee the Father unbegotten; Thee the Only Begotten Son; Thee the Holy Ghost, the Comforter, One Holy and Undivided Trinity with heart and mouth we confess.

℟. We praise Thee, we bless Thee, we glorify Thee; to Thee be glory now and for ever, and world without end. *Amen.*

THE HYMN. *Adesto Sancta Trinitas.*

I.

BE present, Holy Trinity;
Like splendour and one Deity:
Of things above and things below,
Beginning that no end shall know.

ON TRINITY SUNDAY.

II.

Thee all the armies of the sky
Adore, and laud and magnify:
While Nature, in her triple frame,
For ever sanctifies thy name.

III.

And we too, thanks and homage pay,
Thine own adoring flock to-day:
O join to that celestial song
The praises of our suppliant throng!

IV.

To Thee, O Unbegotten One,
And Thee, O Sole-begotten Son,
And Thee, O Holy Ghost, we raise
Our equal and eternal praise.
Amen.

℣. Let us bless the Father, and the Son, and the Holy Ghost.

℟. Praise Him and magnify Him for ever.

From Trinity to Advent, on Saturdays at Vespers, is said the Hymn,
O lux beata Trinitas.

I.

O TRINITY of blessed light,
O Unity of princely might,
The fiery sun now goes his way,
Shed Thou within our hearts thy ray.

II.

To Thee our morning song of praise,
To Thee our evening prayer we raise;
Thy glory suppliant we adore
For ever and for evermore.

III.

All laud to God the Father be;
All praise, Eternal Son, to Thee;
All praise for ever, as is meet,
To God, the Holy Paraclete.
Amen.

℣. Let our evening prayer come up before Thee, O Lord.

℟. And let Thy mercy come down upon us.

III.

THE PSALTER OF THE HOURS:

CONTAINING THE

PSALMS FOR MATINS, PRIME, AND VESPERS,

FOR

SUNDAYS, HOLY DAYS, AND WEEK DAYS

THROUGHOUT THE YEAR.

Sundays and Feast Days.

AT MATINS.

¶ *The Psalms for every Sunday and Feast Day throughout the year, except from Septuagesima to Easter, shall be* 93, 100, 148, 149, 150.

PSALM xciii. *Dominus regnavit.*

THE Lord is King, and hath put on glorious apparel; the Lord hath put on his apparel, and girded himself with strength.

2 He hath made the round world so sure, that it cannot be moved.

3 Ever since the world began, hath thy seat been prepared: thou art from everlasting.

4 The floods are risen, O Lord, the floods have lift up their voice; the floods lift up their waves.

5 The waves of the sea are mighty, and rage horribly; but yet the Lord, who dwelleth on high, is mightier.

6 Thy testimonies, O Lord, are very sure: holiness becometh thine house for ever.

PSALM c. *Jubilate Deo.*

O BE ye joyful in the Lord, all ye lands; serve the Lord with gladness, and come before his presence with a song.

2 Be ye sure that the Lord he is God; it is he that hath made us, and not we ourselves; we are his people, and the sheep of his pasture.

3 O go your way into his gates with thanksgiving, and into his courts with praise; be thankful unto him, and speak good of his name;

4 For the Lord is gracious; his mercy is everlasting; and his truth endureth from generation to generation.

PSALM cxlviii. *Laudate Dominum.*

O PRAISE the Lord of heaven; praise him in the height.

2 Praise him, all ye angels of his; praise him, all his hosts.

3 Praise him, sun and moon; praise him, all ye stars and light.

4 Praise him, all ye heavens, and ye waters that are above the heavens.

5 Let them praise the name of the Lord; for he spake the word, and they were made; he commanded, and they were created.

6 He hath made them fast for ever and ever: he hath given them a law which shall not be broken.

7 Praise the Lord upon earth: ye dragons and all deeps.

8 Fire and hail, snow and vapours, wind and storm, fulfilling his word:

9 Mountains and all hills; fruitful trees and all cedars:

10 Beasts and all cattle; worms and feathered fowls:

11 Kings of the earth, and all people; princes, and all judges of the world:

12 Young men and maidens, old men and children, praise the Name of the Lord: for his

Name only is excellent, and his praise above heaven and earth.

13 He shall exalt the horn of his people: all his saints shall praise him; even the children of Israel, even the people that serveth him.

PSALM cxlix. *Cantate Domino.*

O SING unto the Lord a new song; let the congregation of saints praise him.

2 Let Israel rejoice in him that made him, and let the children of Sion be joyful in their King.

3 Let them praise his Name in the dance: let them sing praises unto him with tabret and harp.

4 For the Lord hath pleasure in his people, and helpeth the meek-hearted.

5 Let the saints be joyful with glory; let them rejoice in their beds.

6 Let the praises of God be in their mouth; and a two-edged sword in their hands.

7 To be avenged of the heathen, and to rebuke the people;

8 To bind their kings in chains, and their nobles with links of iron.

9. That they may be avenged of them; as it is written, Such honour have all his saints.

PSALM cl. *Laudate Dominum.*

O PRAISE God in his holiness: praise him in the firmament of his power.

2 Praise him in his noble acts: praise him according to his excellent greatness.

3 Praise him in the sound of the trumpet; praise him upon the lute and harp.

4 Praise him in the cymbals and dances: praise him upon the strings and pipe.

5 Praise him upon the well-tuned cymbals: praise him upon the loud cymbals.

6 Let every thing that hath breath praise the Lord.

¶ *From Septuagesima to Easter, instead of Ps. 98, shall be said Ps. 51, and instead of Ps. 100, shall be said Ps. 87, as follows:*

PSALM li. *Miserere mei, Deus.*

HAVE mercy upon me, O God, after thy great goodness; according to the multitude of thy mercies, do away mine offences.

2 Wash me thoroughly from my wickedness, and cleanse me from my sin;

3 For I acknowledge my faults, and my sin is ever before me.

4 Against thee only have I sinned, and done this evil in thy sight, that thou mightest be justified in thy saying, and clear when thou art judged.

5 Behold I was shapen in wickedness, and in sin hath my mother conceived me.

6 But lo, thou requirest truth in the inward parts, and shalt make me to understand wisdom secretly.

7 Thou shalt purge me with hyssop, and I shall be clean; thou shalt wash me, and I shall be whiter than snow.

8 Thou shalt make me hear of joy and gladness, that the bones which thou hast broken may rejoice.

9 Turn thy face from my sins, and put out all my misdeeds.

10 Make me a clean heart, O God, and renew a right spirit within me.

11 Cast me not away from thy presence, and take not thy holy Spirit from me.

12 O give me the comfort of thy help again, and stablish me with thy free Spirit.

13 Then shall I teach thy ways unto the wicked, and sinners shall be converted unto thee.

14 Deliver me from bloodguiltiness, O God, thou that art the God of my health; and my tongue shall sing of thy righteousness.

15 Thou shalt open my lips, O Lord, and my mouth shall show thy praise.

16 For thou desirest no sacrifice, else would I give it thee; but thou delightest not in burnt-offerings.

17 The sacrifice of God, is a troubled spirit; a broken and contrite heart, O God, shalt thou not despise.

18 O be favourable and gracious unto Sion; build thou the walls of Jerusalem.

19 Then shalt thou be pleased with the sacrifice of righteousness, with the burnt-offerings and oblations; then shall they offer young bullocks upon thine altar.

PSALM lxxxvii. *Fundamenta ejus.*

HER foundations are upon the holy hills: the Lord loveth the gates of Sion more than all the dwellings of Jacob.

2 Very excellent things are spoken of thee, thou city of God.

3 I will think upon Rahab and Babylon, with them that know me.

4 Behold ye the Philistines also, and they of Tyre, with the Morians; lo, there was he born.

5 And of Sion it shall be reported that he was born in her; and the Most High shall stablish her.

6 The Lord shall rehearse it, when he writeth up the people, that he was born there.

7 The singers also and trumpeters shall he rehearse: All my fresh springs shall be in thee.

¶ *Then shall follow* Ps. 148, 149, 150, *as before.*

AT PRIME.

¶ *From Advent to Septuagesima shall be sung* Ps. 19, *on all Sundays and Feast days.*

PSALM xix. *Cæli enarrant.*

THE heavens declare the glory of God; and the firmament showeth his handy work.

2 One day telleth another; and one night certifieth another.

3 There is neither speech nor language; but their voices are heard among them.

4 Their sound is gone out into all lands; and their words into the ends of the world.

5 In them hath he set a tabernacle for the sun; which cometh forth as a bridegroom out of his chamber, and rejoiceth as a giant to run his course.

6 It goeth forth from the uttermost part of the heaven, and runneth about unto the end of it again; and there is nothing hid from the heat thereof.

7 The law of the Lord is an undefiled law, converting the soul; the testimony of the Lord is sure, and giveth wisdom unto the simple.

8 The statutes of the Lord are right, and rejoice the heart; the commandment of the Lord is pure, and giveth light unto the eyes.

9 The fear of the Lord is clean, and endureth for ever; the judgments of the Lord are true, and righteous altogether.

10 More to be desired are they than gold, yea, than much fine gold; sweeter also than honey, and the honey-comb.

11 Moreover, by them is thy servant taught; and in keeping of them there is great reward.

12 Who can tell how oft he offendeth? O cleanse thou me from my secret faults.

13 Keep thy servant also from presumptuous sins, lest they get the dominion over me; so shall I be undefiled, and innocent from the great offence.

14 Let the words of my mouth, and the meditation of my heart, be alway acceptable in thy sight,

15 O Lord, my strength, and my Redeemer.

¶ *From Septuagesima to Easter, and from Trinity Sunday to Advent, Ps. 63.*

PSALM lxiii. *Deus, Deus meus.*

O GOD, thou art my God; early will I seek thee.

2 My soul thirsteth for thee; my flesh also longeth after thee, in a barren and dry land where no water is.

3 Thus have I looked for thee in holiness, that I might behold thy power and glory.

4 For thy loving-kindness is better than the life itself: my lips shall praise thee.

5 As long as I live will I magnify thee in this manner, and lift up my hands in thy Name.

6 My soul shall be satisfied, even as it were with marrow and fatness, when my mouth praiseth thee with joyful lips.

7 Have I not remembered thee in my bed, and thought upon thee when I was waking?

8 Because thou hast been my helper; therefore under the shadow of thy wings will I rejoice.

9 My soul hangeth upon thee; thy right hand hath upholden me.

10 These also that seek the hurt of my soul, they shall go under the earth.

11 Let them fall upon the edge of the sword, that they may be a portion for foxes.

12 But the King shall rejoice in God; all they also that swear by him shall be commended; for the mouth of them that speak lies shall be stopped.

¶ *From Easter Day to Trinity Sunday.*

PSALM ii. *Quare fremuerunt gentes?*

WHY do the heathen so furiously rage together? and why do the people imagine a vain thing?

2 The kings of the earth stand up, and the rulers take counsel together against the Lord, and against his Anointed:

3 Let us break their bonds asunder, and cast away their cords from us.

4 He that dwelleth in heaven shall laugh them to scorn: the Lord shall have them in derision.

5 Then shall he speak unto them in his wrath, and vex them in his sore displeasure.

6 Yet have I set my King upon my holy hill of Sion.

7 I will preach the law whereof the Lord hath said unto me, Thou art my Son, this day have I begotten thee.

8 Desire of me, and I shall give thee the heathen for thine inheritance, and the utmost parts of the earth for thy possession.

9 Thou shalt bruise them with a rod of iron, and break them in pieces like a potter's vessel.

10 Be wise now therefore, O ye kings; be learned, ye that are judges of the earth.

11 Serve the Lord in fear, and rejoice unto him with reverence.

12 Kiss the Son, lest he be angry, and so ye perish from the right way, if his wrath be kindled, yea, but a little. Blessed are all they that put their trust in him.

AT VESPERS.

¶ *The Psalms on all Sundays and Feast Days shall be* 110, 113, 114.

PSALM CX. *Dixit Dominus.*

THE LORD said unto my Lord, Sit thou on my right hand, until I make thine enemies thy footstool.

2 The Lord shall send the rod of thy power out of Sion: be thou ruler, even in the midst among thine enemies.

3 In the day of thy power shall the people offer thee freewill offerings with an holy worship: the dew of thy birth is of the womb of the morning.

4 The Lord sware, and will not repent, Thou art a Priest for ever after the order of Melchizedech.

5 The Lord upon thy right hand shall wound even kings in the day of his wrath.

6 He shall judge among the heathen; he shall fill the places with the dead bodies, and smite in sunder the heads over divers countries.

7 He shall drink of the brook in the way; therefore shall he lift up his head.

PSALM CXIII. *Laudate, pueri.*

PRAISE the Lord, ye servants; O praise the Name of the Lord.

2 Blessed be the Name of the Lord from this time forth for evermore.

3 The Lord's Name is praised from the rising up of the sun unto the going down of the same.

4 The Lord is high above all heathen, and his glory above the heavens.

5 Who is like unto the Lord our God, that hath his dwelling so high, and yet humbleth himself to behold the things that are in heaven and earth!

6 He taketh up the simple out of the dust, and lifteth the poor out of the mire;

7 That he may set him with the princes, even with the princes of his people.

8 He maketh the barren woman to keep house, and to be a joyful mother of children.

PSALM CXIV. *In exitu Israel.*

WHEN Israel came out of Egypt, and the house of Jacob from among the strange people,

2 Judah was his sanctuary, and Israel his dominion.

3 The sea saw that, and fled; Jordan was driven back.

4 The mountains skipped like rams, and the little hills like young sheep.

5 What aileth thee, O thou

sea, that thou fleddest? and thou Jordan, that thou wast driven back?

6 Ye mountains, that ye skipped like rams? and ye little hills, like young sheep?

7 Tremble, thou earth at the presence of the Lord; at the presence of the God of Jacob;

8 Who turned the hard rock into a standing water, and the flint-stone into a springing well.

Monday.

AT MATINS.

¶ *From Advent to Septuagesima, and from Easter Day to Trinity Sunday, Ps. 8, 148.*

PSALM viii. *Domine, Dominus noster.*

O LORD, our Governor, how excellent is thy name in all the world; thou that hast set thy glory above the heavens!

2 Out of the mouth of very babes and sucklings hast thou ordained strength, because of thine enemies, that thou mightest still the enemy and the avenger.

3 For I will consider thy heavens, even the works of thy fingers; the moon and the stars which thou hast ordained.

4 What is man, that thou art mindful of him? and the son of man that thou visitest him?

5 Thou madest him lower than the angels, to crown him with glory and worship.

6 Thou makest him to have dominion of the works of thy hands: and thou hast put all things in subjection under his feet;

7 All sheep and oxen; yea, and the beasts of the field;

8 The fowls of the air, and the fishes of the sea; and whatsoever walketh through the paths of the seas.

9 O Lord, our Governor, how excellent is thy name in all the world!

(*For Ps. 148, see page 75 of the Psalter.*)

¶ *From Septuagesima to Easter Day, Ps. 57 shall be said, instead of Ps. 8.*

PSALM lvii. *Miserere mei, Deus.*

BE merciful unto me, O God, be merciful unto me; for my soul trusteth in thee; and under the shadow of thy wings shall be my refuge, until this tyranny be overpast.

2 I will call unto the most high God, even unto the God that shall perform the cause which I have in hand.

3 He shall send from heaven, and save me from the reproof of him that would eat me up.

4 God shall send forth his mercy and truth: my soul is among lions.

5 And I lie even among the children of men, that are set on fire, whose teeth are spears and arrows, and their tongue a sharp sword.

6 Set up thyself, O God, above the heavens; and thy glory above all the earth.

7 They have laid a net for my feet, and pressed down my soul; they have digged a pit before me, and are fallen into the midst of it themselves.

8 My heart is fixed, O God, my heart is fixed; I will sing and give praise.

9 Awake up, my glory; awake, lute and harp: I myself will awake right early.

10 I will give thanks unto thee, O Lord, among the people; and I will sing unto thee among the nations.

11 For the greatness of thy mercy reacheth unto the heavens, and thy truth unto the clouds.

12 Set up thyself, O God, above the heavens; and thy glory above all the earth.

¶ *Then shall follow* Ps. 148, *as before.*

¶ *From Trinity Sunday to Advent,* Ps. 5, 150.

PSALM V. *Verba mea auribus.*

PONDER my words, O Lord, consider my meditation.

2 O hearken thou unto the voice of my calling, my King, and my God: for unto thee will I make my prayer.

3 My voice shalt thou hear betimes, O Lord; early in the morning will I direct my prayer unto thee, and will look up.

4 For thou art the God that hast no pleasure in wickedness; neither shall any evil dwell with thee.

5 Such as be foolish, shall not stand in thy sight; for thou hatest all them that work vanity.

6 Thou shalt destroy them that speak lies: the Lord will abhor both the blood-thirsty and deceitful man.

7 But as for me, I will come into thine house, even upon the multitude of thy mercy, and in thy fear will I worship toward thy holy temple.

8 Lead me, O Lord, in thy righteousness, because of mine enemies; make thy way plain before my face.

9 For there is no faithfulness in his mouth; their inward parts are very wickedness.

10 Their throat is an open sepulchre; they flatter with their tongue.

11 Destroy thou them, O God; let them perish through their own imaginations; cast them out in the multitude of their ungodliness; for they have rebelled against thee.

12 And let all them that put their trust in thee rejoice: they shall ever be giving of thanks, because thou defendest them; they that love thy name shall be joyful in thee.

13 For thou, Lord, wilt give thy blessing unto the righteous, and with thy favourable kindness wilt thou defend him as with a shield.

PSALM cl. *Laudate Dominum.*

O PRAISE God in his holiness; praise him in the firmament of his power.

2 Praise him in his noble acts; praise him according to his excellent greatness.

3 Praise him in the sound of the trumpet; praise him upon the lute and harp.

4 Praise him in the cymbals and dances; praise him upon the strings and pipe.

5 Praise him upon the well-tuned cymbals; praise him upon the loud cymbals.

6 Let every thing that hath breath praise the Lord.

AT PRIME.

¶ *From Advent to Septuagesima, and from Easter to Trinity Monday*, Ps. 48.

PSALM xlviii. *Magnus Dominus.*

GREAT is the Lord, and highly to be praised in the city of our God, even upon his holy hill.

2 The hill of Sion is a fair place, and the joy of the whole earth; upon the north side lieth the city of the great King: God is well known in her palaces as a sure refuge.

3 For lo, the kings of the earth are gathered, and gone by together.

4 They marvelled to see such things; they were astonished, and suddenly cast down.

5 Fear came there upon them; and sorrow, as upon a woman in her travail.

6 Thou shalt break the ships of the sea through the east wind.

7 Like as we have heard, so have we seen in the city of the Lord of hosts, in the city of our God; God upholdeth the same for ever.

8 We wait for thy lovingkindness, O God, in the midst of thy temple.

9 O God, according to thy name, so is thy praise unto the world's end; thy right hand is full of righteousness.

10 Let the mount Sion rejoice, and the daughter of Judah be glad, because of thy judgments.

11 Walk about Sion, and go round about her; and tell the towers thereof.

12 Mark well her bulwarks, set up her houses, that ye may tell them that come after.

13 For this God is our God for ever and ever: He shall be our guide unto death.

¶ *From Septuagesima to Easter*, Ps. 55.

PSALM lv. *Exaudi, Deus.*

HEAR my prayer, O God, and hide not thyself from my petition.

2 Take heed unto me, and hear me, how I mourn in my prayer, and am vexed.

3 The enemy crieth so, and the ungodly cometh on so fast; for they are minded to do me some mischief, so maliciously are they set against me.

4 My heart is disquieted within me, and the fear of death is fallen upon me.

5 Fearfulness and trembling are come upon me, and an horrible dread hath overwhelmed me.

6 And I said, O that I had wings like a dove! for then would I flee away, and be at rest.

7 Lo, then would I get me away far off, and remain in the wilderness.

8 I would make haste to escape, because of the stormy wind and tempest.

9 Destroy their tongues, O Lord, and divide them; for I have spied unrighteousness and strife in the city.

10 Day and night they go about within the walls thereof; mischief also and sorrow are in the midst of it.

11 Wickedness is therein; deceit and guile go not out of their streets.

12 For it is not an open enemy that hath done me this dishonour; for then I could have borne it:

13 Neither was it mine adversary that did magnify himself against me ; for then peradventure I would have hid myself from him :

14 But it was even thou, my companion, my guide, and mine own familiar friend.

15 We took sweet counsel together, and walked in the house of God as friends.

16 Let death come hastily upon them, and let them go down quick into hell ; for wickedness is in their dwellings, and among them.

17 As for me, I will call upon God, and the Lord shall save me.

18 In the evening, and morning, and at noon-day, will I pray, and that instantly ; and he shall hear my voice.

19 It is he that hath delivered my soul in peace, from the battle that was against me ; for there were many with me.

20 Yea, even God that endureth for ever, shall hear me, and bring them down ; for they will not turn, nor fear God.

21 He laid his hands upon such as be at peace with him, and he brake his covenant.

22 The words of his mouth were softer than butter, having war in his heart ; his words were smoother than oil, and yet be they very swords.

23 O cast thy burden upon the Lord, and he shall nourish thee, and shall not suffer the righteous to fall for ever.

24 And as for them, thou, O God, shalt bring them into the pit of destruction.

25 The blood-thirsty and deceitful men shall not live out half their days : nevertheless, my trust shall be in thee, O Lord.

¶ *From Trinity Monday to Advent,* Ps. 119, 1–16.

PSALM cxix. *Beati immaculati.*

BLESSED are those that are undefiled in the way, and walk in the law of the Lord.

2 Blessed are they that keep his testimonies, and seek him with their whole heart.

3 For they who do no wickedness, walk in his ways.

4 Thou hast charged, that we shall diligently keep thy commandments.

5 O that my ways were made so direct, that I might keep thy statutes !

6 So shall I not be confounded, while I have respect unto all thy commandments.

7 I will thank thee with an unfeigned heart, when I shall have learned the judgments of thy righteousness.

8 I will keep thy ceremonies ; O forsake me not utterly.

In quo corriget ?

WHEREWITHAL shall a young man cleanse his way ? even by ruling himself after thy word.

2 With my whole heart have I sought thee ; O let me not go wrong out of thy commandments !

3 Thy words have I hid within my heart, that I should not sin against thee.

4 Blessed art thou, O Lord ; O teach me thy statutes.

5 With my lips have I been telling of all the judgments of thy mouth.

6 I have had as great delight

in the way of thy testimonies, as in all manner of riches.

7 ¶ I will talk of thy commandments, and have respect unto thy ways.

8 My delight shall be in thy statutes, and I will not forget thy word.

AT VESPERS.

PSALM CXX. *Ad Dominum.*

WHEN I was in trouble, I called upon the Lord, and he heard me.

2 Deliver my soul, O Lord, from lying lips, and from a deceitful tongue.

3 What reward shall be given or done unto thee, thou false tongue? even mighty and sharp arrows, with hot burning coals.

4 Woe is me, that I am constrained to dwell with Mesech, and to have my habitation among the tents of Kedar!

5 My soul hath long dwelt among them that are enemies unto peace.

6 I labour for peace; but when I speak unto them thereof, they make them ready to battle.

PSALM CXXI. *Levavi oculos meos.*

I WILL lift up mine eyes unto the hills, from whence cometh my help.

2 My help cometh even from the Lord, who hath made heaven and earth.

3 He will not suffer thy foot to be moved; and he that keepeth thee will not sleep.

4 Behold, he that keepeth Israel shall neither slumber nor sleep.

5 The Lord himself is thy keeper; the Lord is thy defence upon thy right hand;

6 So that the sun shall not burn thee by day, neither the moon by night.

7 The Lord shall preserve thee from all evil; yea, it is even he that shall keep thy soul.

8 The Lord shall preserve thy going out, and thy coming in, from this time forth for evermore.

PSALM CXXII. *Lætatus sum.*

I WAS glad when they said unto me, We will go into the house of the Lord.

2 Our feet shall stand in thy gates, O Jerusalem.

3 Jerusalem is built as a city that is at unity in itself.

4 For thither the tribes go up, even the tribes of the Lord, to testify unto Israel, to give thanks unto the Name of the Lord.

5 For there is the seat of judgment, even the seat of the house of David.

6 O pray for the peace of Jerusalem; they shall prosper that love thee.

7 Peace be within thy walls, and plenteousness within thy palaces.

8 For my brethren and companions' sakes, I will wish thee prosperity.

9 Yea, because of the house of the Lord our God, I will seek to do thee good.

Tuesday.

AT MATINS.

¶ *From Advent to Septuagesima, and from Easter Day to Trinity Monday*, Ps. 24, 148.

PSALM xxiv. *Domini est terra.*

THE earth is the Lord's, and all that therein is; the compass of the world, and they that dwell therein.

2 For he hath founded it upon the seas, and prepared it upon the floods.

3 Who shall ascend into the hill of the Lord? or who shall rise up in his holy place?

4 Even he that hath clean hands, and a pure heart; and that hath not lift up his mind unto vanity, nor sworn to deceive his neighbour.

5 He shall receive the blessing from the Lord, and righteousness from the God of his salvation.

6 This is the generation of them that seek him, even of them that seek thy face, O Jacob.

7 Lift up your heads, O ye gates; and be ye lift up, ye everlasting doors; and the King of glory shall come in.

8 Who is the King of glory? It is the Lord strong and mighty, even the Lord mighty in battle.

9 Lift up your heads, O ye gates; and be ye lift up, ye everlasting doors; and the King of glory shall come in.

10 Who is the King of glory? even the Lord of hosts, he is the King of glory.

(*For* Ps. 148, *see page* 75.)

¶ *From Septuagesima to Easter.* Ps. 54, 148.

PSALM liv. *Deus, in nomine.*

SAVE me, O God, for thy name's sake, and avenge me in thy strength.

2 Hear my prayer, O God, and hearken unto the words of my mouth:

3 For strangers are risen up against me; and tyrants, which have not God before their eyes, seek after my soul.

4 Behold, God is my helper; the Lord is with them that uphold my soul.

5 He shall reward evil unto mine enemies: destroy thou them in thy truth.

6 An offering of a free heart will I give thee, and praise thy name, O Lord; because it is so comfortable.

7 For he hath delivered me out of all my trouble; and mine eye hath seen his desire upon mine enemies.

¶ *From Trinity to Advent*, Ps. 99, 150. (*For* Ps. 150, *see page* 81.)

PSALM xcix. *Dominus regnavit.*

THE Lord is king, be the people never so impatient; he sitteth between the cherubim, be the earth never so unquiet.

2 The Lord is great in Sion, and high above all people.

3 They shall give thanks unto thy name, which is great, wonderful, and holy.

4 The king's power loveth judgment; thou hast prepared

equity; thou hast executed judgment and righteousness in Jacob.

5 O magnify the Lord our God, and fall down before his footstool; for he is holy.

6 Moses and Aaron among his priests, and Samuel among such as call upon his name; these called upon the Lord, and he heard them.

7 He spake unto them out of the cloudy pillar; for they kept his testimonies, and the law that he gave them.

8 Thou heardest them, O Lord our God; thou forgavest them, O God, and punishedst their own inventions.

9 O magnify the Lord our God, and worship him upon his holy hill; for the Lord our God is holy.

AT PRIME.

¶ *From Advent to Septuagesima, and from Easter to Trinity Monday,* Ps. 85.

PSALM lxxxv. *Benedixisti, Domine.*

LORD, thou art become gracious unto thy land; thou hast turned away the captivity of Jacob.

2 Thou hast forgiven the offence of thy people, and covered all their sins.

3 Thou hast taken away all thy displeasure, and turned thyself from thy wrathful indignation.

4 Turn us then, O God our Saviour, and let thine anger cease from us.

5 Wilt thou be displeased at us for ever? and wilt thou stretch out thy wrath from one generation to another?

6 Wilt thou not turn again, and quicken us, that thy people may rejoice in thee?

7 Show us thy mercy, O Lord, and grant us thy salvation.

8 I will hearken what the Lord God will say concerning me; for he shall speak peace unto his people, and to his saints, that they turn not again.

9 For his salvation is nigh them that fear him; that glory may dwell in our land.

10 Mercy and truth are met together: righteousness and peace have kissed each other.

11 Truth shall flourish out of the earth, and righteousness hath looked down from heaven.

12 Yea, the Lord shall show loving-kindness; and our land shall give her increase.

13 Righteousness shall go before him; and he shall direct his going in the way.

¶ *From Septuagesima to Easter,* Ps. 3.

PSALM iii. *Domine, quid multiplicati!*

LORD, how are they increased that trouble me! many are they that rise against me.

2 Many one there be that say of my soul, There is no help for him in his God.

3 But thou, O Lord, art my defender; thou art my worship, and the lifter up of my head.

4 I did call upon the Lord with my voice, and he heard me out of his holy hill.

5 I laid me down and slept, and rose up again; for the Lord sustained me.

6 I will not be afraid for ten thousands of the people, that have set themselves against me round about.

7 Up, Lord, and help me, O

my God! For thou smitest all mine enemies upon the cheekbone; thou hast broken the teeth of the ungodly.

8 Salvation belongeth unto the Lord; and thy blessing is upon thy people.

¶ *From Trinity Monday to Advent*, Ps. 109, 17–32.

Retribue servo tuo.

O DO well unto thy servant; that I may live and keep thy word.

2 Open thou mine eyes; that I may see the wondrous things of thy law.

3 I am a stranger upon earth; O hide not thy commandments from me!

4 My soul breaketh out for the very fervent desire that it hath alway unto thy judgments.

5 Thou hast rebuked the proud; and cursed are they that do err from thy commandments.

6 O turn from me shame and rebuke; for I have kept thy testimonies.

7 Princes also did sit and speak against me; but thy servant is occupied in thy statutes.

8 For thy testimonies are my delight, and my counsellors.

Adhæsit pavimento.

MY soul cleaveth to the dust; O quicken thou me, according to thy word.

2 I have acknowledged my ways, and thou heardest me: O teach me thy statutes!

3 Make me to understand the way of thy commandments; and so shall I talk of thy wondrous works.

4 My soul melteth away for very heaviness; comfort thou me, according unto thy word.

5 Take from me the way of lying, and cause thou me to make much of thy law.

6 I have chosen the way of truth, and thy judgments have I laid before me.

7 I have stuck unto thy testimonies; O Lord, confound me not!

8 I will run the way of thy commandments, when thou hast set my heart at liberty.

AT VESPERS.

Psalms 123, 124, 125.

PSALM cxxiii. *Ad te levavi oculos meos.*

UNTO thee lift I up mine eyes, O thou that dwellest in the heavens.

2 Behold, even as the eyes of servants look unto the hand of their masters, and as the eyes of a maiden unto the hand of her mistress, even so our eyes wait upon the Lord our God, until he have mercy upon us.

3 Have mercy upon us, O Lord, have mercy upon us; for we are utterly despised.

4 Our soul is filled with the scornful reproof of the wealthy, and with the despitefulness of the proud.

PSALM cxxiv. *Nisi quia Dominus.*

IF the Lord himself had not been on our side, now may Israel say; if the Lord himself had not been on our side, when men rose up against us;

2 They had swallowed us up quick; when they were so wrathfully displeased at us.

3 Yea, the waters had drowned us, and the stream had gone over our soul.

4 The deep waters of the proud had gone even over our soul.

5 But praised be the Lord, who hath not given us over for a prey unto their teeth.

6 Our soul is escaped even as a bird out of the snare of the fowler; the snare is broken and we are delivered.

7 Our help standeth in the name of the Lord, who hath made heaven and earth.

PSALM CXXV. *Qui confidunt.*

THEY that put their trust in the Lord shall be even as the mount Sion, which may not be removed, but standeth fast for ever.

2 The hills stand about Jerusalem; even so standeth the Lord round about his people, from this time forth for evermore.

3 For the rod of the ungodly cometh not unto the lot of the righteous; lest the righteous put their hand unto wickedness.

4 Do well, O Lord, unto those that are good and true of heart.

5 As for such as turn back unto their own wickedness, the Lord shall lead them forth with the evil doers; but peace shall be upon Israel.

Wednesday.

AT MATINS.

¶ *From Advent to Septuagesima, and from Easter to Trinity Monday.* Ps. 47, 148.

PSALM xlvii. *Omnes Gentes, plaudite.*

O CLAP your hands together, all ye people: O sing unto God with the voice of melody.

2 For the Lord is high, and to be feared; he is the great King upon all the earth.

3 He shall subdue the people under us, and the nations under our feet.

4 He shall choose out a heritage for us, even the worship of Jacob, whom he loved.

5 God is gone up with a merry noise, and the Lord with the sound of the trump.

6 O sing praises, sing praises unto our God; O sing praises, sing praises unto our King.

7 For God is the King of all the earth: sing ye praises with understanding.

8 God reigneth over the heathen; God sitteth upon his holy seat.

9 The princes of the people are joined unto the people of the God of Abraham; for God, which is very high exalted, doth defend the earth as it were with a shield.

¶ *From Septuagesima to Easter,* Ps. 42, 148.

PSALM xlii. *Quemadmodum.*

LIKE as the hart desireth the water-brooks, so longeth my soul after thee, O God.

2 My soul is athirst for God, yea, even for the living God: when shall I come to appear before the presence of God?

8 My tears have been my meat day and night; while they daily say unto me, Where is now thy God?

4 Now when I think thereupon, I pour out my heart by myself; for I went with the multitude, and brought them forth into the house of God;

5 In the voice of praise and thanksgiving, among such as keep holy-day.

6 Why art thou so full of heaviness, O my soul? and why art thou so disquieted within me?

7 Put thy trust in God; for I will yet give him thanks for the help of his countenance.

8 My God, my soul is vexed within me; therefore will I remember thee concerning the land of Jordan, and the little hill of Hermon.

9 One deep calleth another, because of the noise of the water-pipes; all thy waves and storms are gone over me.

10 The Lord hath granted his loving-kindness in the daytime; and in the night season did I sing of him, and made my prayer unto the God of my life.

11 I will say unto the God of my strength, Why hast thou forgotten me? Why go I thus heavily, while the enemy oppresseth me?

12 My bones are smitten asunder as with a sword, while mine enemies that trouble me cast me in the teeth;

13 Namely, while they say daily unto me, Where is now thy God?

14 Why art thou so vexed, O my soul? and why art thou so disquieted within me?

15 O put thy trust in God; for I will yet thank him, which is the help of my countenance, and my God.

¶ *From Trinity Monday to Advent, Ps. 41, 148.*

PSALM xli. *Beatus qui intelligit.*

BLESSED is he that considereth the poor and needy; the Lord shall deliver him in the time of trouble.

2 The Lord preserve him, and keep him alive, that he may be blessed upon earth; and deliver not thou him into the will of his enemies.

3 The Lord comfort him when he lieth sick upon his bed; make thou all his bed in his sickness.

4 I said, Lord, be merciful unto me; heal my soul, for I have sinned against thee.

5 Mine enemies speak evil of me, When shall he die, and his name perish?

6 And if he come to see me, he speaketh vanity, and his heart conceiveth falsehood within himself; and when he cometh forth, he telleth it.

7 All mine enemies whisper together against me; even against me do they imagine this evil.

8 Let the sentence of guiltiness proceed against him; and now that he lieth, let him rise up no more.

9 Yea, even mine own familiar friend whom I trusted, who did also eat of my bread, hath laid great weight for me.

10 But be thou merciful unto me, O Lord; raise thou me up again, and I shall reward them.

11 By this I know thou favourest me, that mine enemy doth not triumph against me.

12 And when I am in my health, thou upholdest me, and shalt set me before thy face for ever.

13 Blessed be the Lord God of Israel, world without end. Amen.

AT PRIME.

¶ *From Advent to Septuagesima, and from Easter to Trinity Monday, Ps. 33, 1-11.*

PSALM xxxiii. *Exultate, justi.*

REJOICE in the Lord, O ye righteous; for it becometh well the just to be thankful.

2 Praise the Lord with harp; sing praises unto him with the lute, and instrument of ten strings.

3 Sing unto the Lord a new song; sing praises lustily unto him with a good courage;

4 For the word of the Lord is true, and all his works are faithful.

5 He loveth righteousness and judgment; the earth is full of the goodness of the Lord.

6 By the word of the Lord were the heavens made, and all the hosts of them by the breath of his mouth.

7 He gathereth the waters of the sea together, as it were upon a heap; and layeth up the deep as in a treasure-house.

8 Let all the earth fear the Lord; stand in awe of him, all ye that dwell in the world;

9 For he spake, and it was done; he commanded, and it stood fast.

10 The Lord bringeth the counsel of the heathen to naught, and maketh the devices of the people to be of none effect, and casteth out the counsels of princes.

11 The counsel of the Lord shall endure for ever, and the thoughts of his heart from generation to generation.

¶ *From Septuagesima to Easter, Ps. 12, 13.*

PSALM xii. *Salvum me fac.*

HELP me, Lord, for there is not one godly man left; for the faithful are minished from among the children of men.

2 They talk of vanity every one with his neighbour; they do but flatter with their lips, and dissemble in their double heart.

3 The Lord shall root out all deceitful lips, and the tongue that speaketh proud things:

4 Which have said, With our tongue will we prevail; we are they that ought to speak: who is Lord over us?

5 Now, for the comfortless troubles' sake of the needy, and because of the deep sighing of the poor,

6 I will up, saith the Lord, and will help every one from him that swelleth against him, and will set him at rest.

7 The words of the Lord are pure words, even as the silver which from the earth is tried, and purified seven times in the fire.

8 Thou shalt keep them, O Lord; thou shalt preserve him from this generation for ever.

9 The ungodly walk on every side: when they are exalted, the children of men are put to rebuke.

PSALM xiii. *Usque quo, Domine?*

HOW long wilt thou forget me, O Lord; for ever? how long wilt thou hide thy face from me?

2 How long shall I seek coun-

sel in my soul, and be so vexed in my heart? How long shall mine enemies triumph over me?

3 Consider, and hear me, O Lord my God; lighten mine eyes, that I sleep not in death;

4 Lest mine enemy say, I have prevailed against him: for if I be cast down, they that trouble me will rejoice at it.

5 But my trust is in thy mercy, and my heart is joyful in thy salvation.

6 I will sing of the Lord, because he hath dealt so lovingly with me; yea, I will praise the Name of the Lord most highest.

¶ *From Trinity Monday to Advent,* Ps. 119, 49–64.

Memor esto servi tui.

O THINK upon thy servant, as concerning thy word, wherein thou hast caused me to put my trust.

2 The same is my comfort in my trouble; for thy word hath quickened me.

3 The proud have had me exceedingly in derision; yet have I not shrinked from thy law.

4 For I remembered thine everlasting judgments, O Lord, and received comfort.

5 I am horribly afraid, for the ungodly that forsake thy law.

6 Thy statutes have been my songs, in the house of my pilgrimage.

7 I have thought upon thy name, O Lord, in the night season, and have kept thy law.

8 This I had, because I kept thy commandments.

Portio mea, Domine.

THOU art my portion, O Lord; I have promised to keep thy law.

2 I made my humble petition in thy presence with my whole heart; O be merciful unto me, according to thy word.

3 I called mine own ways to remembrance, and turned my feet unto thy testimonies.

4 I made haste, and prolonged not the time, to keep thy commandments.

5 The congregations of the ungodly have robbed me; but I have not forgotten thy law.

6 At midnight I will rise to give thanks unto thee; because of thy righteous judgments.

7 I am a companion of all them that fear thee, and keep thy commandments.

8 The earth, O Lord, is full of thy mercy: O teach me thy statutes!

AT VESPERS.

Psalms 126, 127, 128.

PSALM cxxvi. *In convertendo.*

WHEN the Lord turned again the captivity of Sion, then were we like unto them that dream.

2 Then was our mouth filled with laughter, and our tongue with joy.

3 Then said they among the heathen, the Lord hath done great things for them.

4 Yea, the Lord hath done great things for us already; whereof we rejoice.

5 Turn our captivity, O Lord, as the rivers in the south.

6 They that sow in tears, shall reap in joy.

7 He that now goeth on his way weeping, and beareth forth good seed, shall doubtless come again with joy, and bring his sheaves with him.

THE PSALTER.

Psalm cxxvii. *Nisi Dominus.*

EXCEPT the Lord build the house, their labor is but lost that build it.

2 Except the Lord keep the city, the watchman waketh but in vain.

3 It is but lost labour that ye haste to rise up early, and so late take rest, and eat the bread of carefulness; for so he giveth his beloved sleep.

4 Lo, children and the fruit of the womb are a heritage and gift that cometh of the Lord.

5 Like as the arrows in the hand of the giant, even so are the young children.

6 Happy is the man that hath his quiver full of them; they shall not be ashamed when they speak with their enemies in the gate.

Psalm cxxviii. *Beati omnes.*

BLESSED are all they that fear the Lord, and walk in his ways.

2 For thou shalt eat the labour of thine hands: O well is thee, and happy shalt thou be!

3 Thy wife shall be as the fruitful vine upon the walls of thine house.

4 Thy children like the olive branches, round about thy table.

5 Lo, thus shall the man be blessed that feareth the Lord.

6 The Lord from out of Sion shall so bless thee, that thou shalt see Jerusalem in prosperity all thy life long;

7 Yea, that thou shalt see thy children's children, and peace upon Israel.

Thursday.

AT MATINS.

¶ *From Advent to Septuagesima, and from Easter to Trinity Monday*, Ps. 97, 148.

Psalm xcvii. *Dominus regnavit.*

THE Lord is King, the earth may be glad thereof; yea, the multitude of the isles may be glad thereof.

2 Clouds and darkness are round about him: righteousness and judgment are the habitation of his seat.

3 There shall go a fire before him, and burn up his enemies on every side.

4 His lightnings gave shine unto the world: the earth saw it, and was afraid.

5 The hills melted like wax at the presence of the Lord; at the presence of the Lord of the whole earth.

6 The heavens have declared his righteousness, and all the people have seen his glory.

7 Confounded be all they that worship carved images, and that delight in vain gods: worship him, all ye gods.

8 Sion heard of it, and rejoiced; and the daughters of Judah were glad, because of thy judgments, O Lord.

9 For thou, Lord, art higher than all that are in the earth: thou art exalted far above all gods.

10 O ye that love the Lord, see that ye hate the thing which is evil: the Lord preserveth the souls of his saints; he shall de-

liver them from the hand of the ungodly.

11 There is sprung up a light for the righteous, and joyful gladness for such as are true-hearted.

12 Rejoice in the Lord, ye righteous; and give thanks for a remembrance of his holiness.

¶ *From Septuagesima to Easter,* Ps. 117, 148.

PSALM cxvii. *Laudate Dominum.*

O PRAISE the Lord, all ye heathen; praise him, all ye nations.

2 For his merciful kindness is ever more and more towards us; and the truth of the Lord endureth for ever. Praise the Lord.

¶ *From Trinity Monday to Advent,* Ps. 96, 150.

PSALM xcvi. *Cantate Domino.*

O SING unto the Lord a new song; sing unto the Lord, all the whole earth.

2 Sing unto the Lord, and praise his name; be telling of his salvation from day to day.

3 Declare his honour unto the heathen, and his wonders unto all people.

4 For the Lord is great, and cannot worthily be praised; he is more to be feared than all gods.

5 As for all the gods of the heathen, they are but idols; but it is the Lord that made the heavens.

6 Glory and worship are before him; power and honour are in his sanctuary.

7 Ascribe unto the Lord, O ye kindreds of the people, ascribe unto the Lord worship and power.

8 Ascribe unto the Lord the honour due unto his name; bring presents, and come into his courts.

9 O worship the Lord in the beauty of holiness; let the whole earth stand in awe of him.

10 Tell it out among the heathen, that the Lord is king; and that it is he who hath made the round world so fast that it cannot be moved; and how that he shall judge the people righteously.

11 Let the heavens rejoice, and let the earth be glad; let the sea make a noise, and all that therein is.

12 Let the field be joyful, and all that is in it; then shall all the trees of the wood rejoice before the Lord.

13 For he cometh, for he cometh to judge the earth; and with righteousness to judge the world, and the people with his truth.

AT PRIME.

¶ *From Advent to Septuagesima, and from Easter to Trinity Monday,* Ps. 23.

PSALM xxiii. *Dominus regit me.*

THE Lord is my shepherd; therefore can I lack nothing.

2 He shall feed me in a green pasture, and lead me forth beside the waters of comfort.

3 He shall convert my soul, and bring me forth in the paths of righteousness for his Name's sake.

4 Yea, though I walk through the valley of the shadow of death, I will fear no evil; for thou art with me; thy rod and thy staff comfort me.

5 Thou shalt prepare a table before me against them that trouble me; thou hast anointed

my head with oil, and my cup shall be full.

6 But thy loving-kindness and mercy shall follow me all the days of my life; and I will dwell in the house of the Lord for ever.

¶ *From Septuagesima to Easter,* Ps. 36.

PSALM XXXVI. *Dixit injustus.*

MY heart showeth me the wickedness of the ungodly, that there is no fear of God before his eyes.

2 For he flattereth himself in his own sight, until his abominable sin be found out.

3 The words of his mouth are unrighteous and full of deceit; he hath left off to behave himself wisely, and to do good.

4 He imagineth mischief upon his bed, and hath set himself in no good way; neither doth he abhor any thing that is evil.

5 Thy mercy, O Lord, reacheth unto the heavens, and thy faithfulness unto the clouds.

6 Thy righteousness standeth like the strong mountains: thy judgments are like the great deep.

7 Thou, Lord, shalt save both man and beast: how excellent is thy mercy, O God! and the children of men shall put their trust under the shadow of thy wings.

8 They shall be satisfied with the plenteousness of thy house; and thou shalt give them drink of thy pleasures, as out of the river.

9 For with thee is the well of life; and in thy light shall we see light.

10 O continue forth thy loving-kindness unto them that know thee, and thy righteousness unto them that are true of heart.

11 O let not the foot of pride come against me; and let not the hand of the ungodly cast me down.

12 There are they fallen, all that work wickedness; they are cast down, and shall not be able to stand.

¶ *From Trinity Monday to Advent.* Ps. 119, 65–80.

Bonitatem fecisti.

O LORD, thou hast dealt graciously with thy servant, according unto thy word.

2 O learn me true understanding and knowledge; for I have believed thy commandments.

3 Before I was troubled, I went wrong; but now have I kept thy word.

4 Thou art good and gracious: O teach me thy statutes!

5 The proud have imagined a lie against me; but I will keep thy commandments with my whole heart.

6 Their heart is as fat as brawn; but my delight hath been in thy law.

7 It is good for me that I have been in trouble; that I may learn thy statutes.

8 The law of thy mouth is dearer unto me than thousands of gold and silver.

Manus tuæ fecerunt me.

THY hands have made me, and fashioned me: O give me understanding, that I may learn thy commandments.

2 They that fear thee will be glad when they see me; because I have put my trust in thy word.

3 I know, O Lord, that thy judgments are right, and that thou of very faithfulness hast caused me to be troubled.

4 O let thy merciful kindness be my comfort, according to thy word unto thy servant.

5 O let thy loving mercies come unto me, that I may live; for thy law is my delight.

6 Let the proud be confounded, for they go wickedly about to destroy me; but I will be occupied in thy commandments.

7 Let such as fear thee, and have known thy testimonies, be turned unto me.

8 O let my heart be sound in thy statutes, that I be not ashamed.

AT VESPERS.

Psalms 129, 130, 131.

PSALM CXXIX. *Sæpe expugnaverunt.*

MANY a time have they fought against me from my youth up, may Israel now say:

2 Yea, many a time have they vexed me from my youth up; but they have not prevailed against me.

3 The plowers plowed upon my back, and made long furrows.

4 But the righteous Lord hath hewn the snares of the ungodly in pieces.

5 Let them be confounded and turned backward, as many as have evil will at Sion.

6 Let them be even as the grass growing upon the housetops, which withereth afore it be plucked up;

7 Whereof the mower filleth not his hand, neither he that bindeth up the sheaves his bosom.

8 So that they who go by say not so much as, The Lord prosper you: we wish you good luck in the Name of the Lord.

PSALM CXXX. *De profundis.*

OUT of the deep have I called unto thee, O Lord; Lord, hear my voice.

2 O let thine ears consider well the voice of my complaint.

3 If thou, Lord, wilt be extreme to mark what is done amiss, O Lord, who may abide it?

4 For there is mercy with thee; therefore shalt thou be feared.

5 I look for the Lord; my soul doth wait for him; in his word is my trust.

6 My soul fleeth unto the Lord before the morning watch; I say, before the morning watch.

7 O Israel, trust in the Lord; for with the Lord there is mercy, and with him is plenteous redemption.

8 And he shall redeem Israel from his sins.

PSALM CXXXI. *Domine, non est.*

LORD, I am not high-minded; I have no proud looks.

2 I do not exercise myself in great matters which are too high for me;

3 But I refrain my soul, and keep it low, like as a child that is weaned from his mother: yea, my soul is even as a weaned child.

4 O Israel, trust in the Lord, from this time forth for evermore.

Friday.

AT MATINS.

¶ *From Advent to Septuagesima, and from Easter to Trinity Monday,* Ps. 146, 148.

PSALM cxlvi. *Lauda, anima mea.*

PRAISE the Lord, O my soul: while I live, will I praise the Lord; yea, as long as I have any being, I will sing praises unto my God.

2 O put not your trust in princes, nor in any child of man; for there is no help in them.

3 For when the breath of man goeth forth, he shall turn again to his earth, and then all his thoughts perish.

4 Blessed is he that hath the God of Jacob for his help; and whoso hope is in the Lord his God;

5 Who made heaven and earth, the sea and all that therein is; who keepeth his promise for ever;

6 Who helpeth them to right that suffer wrong; who feedeth the hungry.

7 The Lord looseth men out of prison; the Lord giveth sight to the blind.

8 The Lord helpeth them that are fallen; the Lord careth for the righteous.

9 The Lord careth for the stranger; he defendeth the fatherless and widow: as for the way of the ungodly, he turneth it upside down.

10 The Lord thy God, O Sion, shall be King for evermore, and throughout all generations.

¶ *From Septuagesima to Easter,* Ps. 90, 148.

PSALM xc. *Domine refugium.*

LORD, thou hast been our refuge, from one generation to another.

2 Before the mountains were brought forth, or ever the earth and the world were made, thou art God from everlasting, and world without end.

3 Thou turnest man to destruction; again thou sayest, Come again, ye children of men.

4 For a thousand years in thy sight are but as yesterday; seeing that is past as a watch in the night.

5 As soon as Thou scatterest them they are even as a sleep; and fade away suddenly like the grass.

6 In the morning it is green, and groweth up; but in the evening it is cut down, dried up, and withered.

7 For we consume away in thy displeasure, and are afraid at thy wrathful indignation.

8 Thou hast set our misdeeds before thee; and our secret sins in the light of thy countenance.

9 For when thou art angry all our days are gone: we bring our years to an end, as it were a tale that is told.

10 The days of our age are threescore years and ten; and

though men be so strong that they come to fourscore years, yet is their strength then but labour and sorrow; so soon passeth it away, and we are gone.

11 But who regardeth the power of thy wrath? For even thereafter as a man feareth, so is thy displeasure.

12 So teach us to number our days, that we may apply our hearts unto wisdom.

13 Turn thee again, O Lord, at the last, and be gracious unto thy servants.

14 O satisfy us with thy mercy, and that soon: so shall we rejoice and be glad all the days of our life.

15 Comfort us again now after the time that thou hast plagued us; and for the years wherein we have suffered adversity.

16 Show thy servants thy work, and their children thy glory.

17 And the glorious Majesty of the Lord our God be upon us: prosper thou the work of our hands upon us; O prosper thou our handy-work.

¶ *From Trinity Monday to Advent*, Ps. 64, 150.

PSALM lxiv. *Exaudi, Deus.*

HEAR my voice, O God, in my prayer; preserve my life from fear of the enemy.

2 Hide me from the gathering together of the froward; and from the insurrection of wicked doers;

3 Who have whet their tongue like a sword, and shoot out their arrows, even bitter words;

4 That they may privily shoot at him that is perfect: suddenly do they hit him, and fear not.

5 They encourage themselves in mischief, and commune among themselves, how they may lay snares; and say, that no man shall see them.

6 They imagine wickedness, and practise it; that they keep secret among themselves, every man in the deep of his heart.

7 But God shall suddenly shoot at them with a swift arrow, that they shall be wounded.

8 Yea, their own tongues shall make them fall; insomuch that whoso seeth them shall laugh them to scorn.

9 And all men that see it shall say, This hath God done; for they shall perceive that it is his work.

10 The righteous shall rejoice in the Lord, and put his trust in him; and all they that are true of heart shall be glad.

AT PRIME.

¶ *From Advent to Septuagesima, and from Easter to Trinity Monday*, Ps. 25.

PSALM xxv. *Ad te, Domine, levavi.*

UNTO thee, O Lord, will I lift up my soul; my God, I have put my trust in thee: O let me not be confounded, neither let mine enemies triumph over me.

2 For all they that hope in thee shall not be ashamed; but such as transgress without a cause, shall be put to confusion.

3 Show me thy ways, O Lord, and teach me thy paths.

4 Lead me forth in thy truth, and learn me; for thou art the God of my salvation: in thee

hath been my hope all the day long.

5 Call to remembrance, O Lord, thy tender mercies, and thy loving-kindnesses, which have been ever of old.

6 O remember not the sins and offences of my youth; but according to thy mercy think thou upon me, O Lord, for thy goodness.

7 Gracious and righteous is the Lord; therefore will he teach sinners in the way.

8 Them that are meek shall he guide in judgment; and such as are gentle, them shall he learn his way.

9 All the paths of the Lord are mercy and truth, unto such as keep his covenant and his testimonies.

10 For thy name's sake, O Lord, be merciful unto my sin; for it is great.

11 What man is he that feareth the Lord? him shall he teach in the way that he shall choose.

12 His soul shall dwell at ease, and his seed shall inherit the land.

13 The secret of the Lord is among them that fear him, and he will show them his covenant.

14 Mine eyes are ever looking unto the Lord; for he shall pluck my feet out of the net.

15 Turn thee unto me, and have mercy upon me; for I am desolate, and in misery.

16 The sorrows of my heart are enlarged: O bring thou me out of my troubles.

17 Look upon my adversity and misery, and forgive me all my sin.

18 Consider mine enemies how many they are; and they bear a tyrannous hate against me.

19 O keep my soul, and deliver me: let me not be confounded, for I have put my trust in thee.

20 Let perfectness and righteous dealing wait upon me; for my hope hath been in thee.

21 Deliver Israel, O God, out of all his troubles.

¶ *From Septuagesima to Easter*, Ps. 142.

PSALM cxlii. *Voce mea ad Dominum.*

I CRIED unto the Lord with my voice; yea, even unto the Lord did I make my supplication.

2 I poured out my complaints before him, and showed him of my trouble.

3 When my spirit was in heaviness, thou knewest my path; in the way wherein I walked, have they privily laid a snare for me.

4 I looked also upon my right hand, and saw there was no man that would know me.

5 I had no place to flee unto, and no man cared for my soul.

6 I cried unto thee, O Lord, and said, Thou art my hope, and my portion in the land of the living.

7 Consider my complaint; for I am brought very low.

8 O deliver me from my persecutors, for they are too strong for me.

9 Bring my soul out of prison, that I may give thanks unto thy name; which thing if thou wilt grant me, then shall the righteous resort unto my company.

¶ *From Trinity Monday to Advent*, Ps. 119, 105–120.

Lucerna pedibus meis.

THY word is a lantern unto my feet, and a light unto my paths.

2 I have sworn, and am stedfastly purposed, to keep thy righteous judgments.

3 I am troubled above measure: quicken me, O Lord, according to thy word.

4 Let the free-will offerings of my mouth please thee, O Lord; and teach me thy judgments.

5 My soul is alway in my hand; yet do I not forget thy law.

6 The ungodly have laid a snare for me; but yet I swerved not from thy commandments.

7 Thy testimonies have I claimed as mine heritage for ever; and why? they are the very joy of my heart.

8 I have applied my heart to fulfil thy statutes alway, even unto the end.

Iniquos odio habui.

I HATE them that imagine evil things; but thy law do I love.

2 Thou art my defence and shield; and my trust is in thy word.

3 Away from me, ye wicked; I will keep the commandments of my God.

4 O stablish me according to thy word, that I may live; and let me not be disappointed of my hope.

5 Hold thou me up, and I shall be safe; yea, my delight shall be ever in thy statutes.

6 Thou hast trodden down all them that depart from thy statutes, for they imagine but deceit.

7 Thou puttest away all the ungodly of the earth like dross; therefore I love thy testimonies.

8 My flesh trembleth for fear of thee; and I am afraid of thy judgments.

AT VESPERS.

Psalms 137, 141.

PSALM cxxxvii. *Super flumina.*

BY the waters of Babylon we sat down and wept, when we remembered thee, O Sion.

2 As for our harps, we hanged them up upon the trees that are therein.

3 For they that led us away captive, required of us then a song, and melody in our heaviness: Sing us one of the songs of Sion.

4 How shall we sing the Lord's song in a strange land?

5 If I forget thee, O Jerusalem, let my right hand forget her cunning.

6 If I do not remember thee, let my tongue cleave to the roof of my mouth; yea, if I prefer not Jerusalem in my mirth.

7 Remember the children of Edom, O Lord, in the day of Jerusalem; how they said, Down with it, down with it, even to the ground.

8 O daughter of Babylon, wasted with misery; yea, happy shall he be that rewardeth thee as thou hast served us.

9 Blessed shall he be that taketh thy children, and throweth them against the stones.

PSALM cxli. *Domine, clamavi.*

LORD, I call upon thee; haste thee unto me, and consider my voice, when I cry unto thee.

2 Let my prayer be set forth in thy sight as the incense; and let the lifting up of my hands be an evening sacrifice.
3 Set a watch, O Lord, before my mouth, and keep the door of my lips.
4 O let not mine heart be inclined to any evil thing; let me not be occupied in ungodly works with the men that work wickedness, lest I eat of such things as please them.
5 Let the righteous rather smite me friendly, and reprove me.
6 But let not their precious balms break my head; yea, I will pray yet against their wickedness.
7 Let their judges be overthrown in the stony places, that they may hear my words; for they are sweet.
8 Our bones lie scattered before the pit, like as when one breaketh and heweth wood upon the earth.
9 But mine eyes look unto thee, O Lord God; in thee is my trust; O cast not out my soul.
10 Keep me from the snare that they have laid for me, and from the traps of the wicked doers.
11 Let the ungodly fall into their own nets together: and let me ever escape them.

Saturday.

AT MATINS.

¶ *From Advent to Septuagesima, and from Easter to Trinity Monday,* Ps. 76, 148.

PSALM lxxvi. *Notus in Judæa.*

IN Jewry is God known; his Name is great in Israel.
2 At Salem is his tabernacle, and his dwelling in Sion.
3 There brake he the arrows of the bow, the shield, the sword, and the battle.
4 Thou art of more honour and might than the hills of the robbers.
5 The proud are robbed, they have slept their sleep; and all the men whose hands were mighty have found nothing.
6 At thy rebuke, O God of Jacob, both the chariot and horse are fallen.
7 Thou, even thou art to be feared; and who may stand in thy sight when thou art angry?
8 Thou didst cause thy judgment to be heard from heaven; the earth trembled, and was still,
9 When God arose to judgment, and to help all the meek upon earth.
10 The fierceness of man shall turn to thy praise; and the fierceness of them shalt thou refrain.
11 Promise unto the Lord your God, and keep it, all ye that are round about him; bring presents unto him that ought to be feared.
12 He shall refrain the spirit of princes, and is wonderful among the kings of the earth.

¶ *From Septuagesima to Easter,* Ps. 29, 148.

PSALM xxix. *Afferte Domino.*

BRING unto the Lord, O ye mighty, bring young rams unto the Lord; ascribe unto the Lord worship and strength.

2 Give the Lord the honour due unto his name; worship the Lord with holy worship.

3 It is the Lord that commandeth the waters; it is the glorious God that maketh the thunder.

4 It is the Lord that ruleth the sea; the voice of the Lord is mighty in operation; the voice of the Lord is a glorious voice.

5 The voice of the Lord breaketh the cedar trees; yea, the Lord breaketh the cedars of Libanus.

6 He maketh them also to skip like a calf; Libanus also and Sirion like a young unicorn.

7 The voice of the Lord divideth the flames of fire; the voice of the Lord shaketh the wilderness; yea, the Lord shaketh the wilderness of Cades.

8 The voice of the Lord maketh the hinds to bring forth young, and discovereth the thick bushes: in his temple doth every man speak of his honour.

9 The Lord sitteth above the water flood, and the Lord remaineth a King for ever.

10 The Lord shall give strength unto his people; the Lord shall give his people the blessing of peace.

¶ *From Trinity Monday to Advent,* Ps. 65, 150.

PSALM LXV. *Te decet hymnus.*

THOU, O God, art praised in Sion; and unto thee shall the vow be performed in Jerusalem.

2 Thou that hearest the prayer, unto thee shall all flesh come.

3 My misdeeds prevail against me: O be thou merciful unto our sins.

4 Blessed is the man whom thou choosest, and receivest unto thee: he shall dwell in thy court, and shall be satisfied with the pleasures of thy house, even of thy holy temple.

5 Thou shalt show us wonderful things in thy righteousness, O God of our salvation; thou that art the hope of all the ends of the earth, and of them that remain in the broad sea.

6 Who in his strength setteth fast the mountains, and is girded about with power.

7 Who stilleth the raging of the sea, and the noise of his waves, and the madness of the people.

8 They also that dwell in the uttermost parts of the earth shall be afraid at thy tokens, thou that makest the out-goings of the morning and evening to praise thee.

9 Thou visitest the earth, and blessest it; thou makest it very plenteous.

10 The river of God is full of water: thou preparest their corn, for so thou providest for the earth.

11 Thou waterest her furrows; thou sendest rain into the little valleys thereof; thou makest it soft with the drops of rain, and blessest the increase of it.

12 Thou crownest the year with thy goodness, and thy clouds drop fatness..

13 They shall drop upon the dwellings of the wilderness, and the little hills shall rejoice on every side.

14 The folds shall be full of sheep; the valleys also shall

stand so thick with corn, that they shall laugh and sing.

AT PRIME.

¶ *From Advent to Septuagesima, and from Easter to Trinity Monday*, Ps. 16.

PRESERVE me, O God; for in thee have I put my trust.

2 O my soul, thou hast said unto the Lord, Thou art my God; my goods are nothing unto thee.

3 All my delight is upon the saints that are in the earth, and upon such as excel in virtue.

4 But they that run after another god shall have great trouble.

5 Their drink-offerings of blood will I not offer, neither make mention of their names within my lips.

6 The Lord himself is the portion of mine inheritance and of my cup: thou shalt maintain my lot.

7 The lot is fallen unto me in a fair ground; yea, I have a goodly heritage.

8 I will thank the Lord for giving me warning; my reins also chasten me in the night-season.

9 I have set God alway before me; for he is on my right hand, therefore I shall not fall.

10 Wherefore my heart was glad, and my glory rejoiced: my flesh also shall rest in hope.

11 For why? thou shalt not leave my soul in hell; neither shalt thou suffer thy Holy One to see corruption.

12 Thou shalt show me the path of life: in thy presence is the fulness of joy, and at thy right hand there is pleasure for evermore.

¶ *From Septuagesima to Easter*, Ps. 15.

PSALM XV. *Domine, quis habitabit?*

LORD, who shall dwell in thy tabernacle? or who shall rest upon thy holy hill?

2 Even he that leadeth an uncorrupt life, and doeth the thing which is right, and speaketh the truth from his heart:

3 He that hath used no deceit in his tongue, nor done evil to his neighbour, and hath not slandered his neighbour:

4 He that setteth not by himself, but is lowly in his own eyes, and maketh much of them that fear the Lord:

5 He that sweareth unto his neighbour, and disappointeth him not, though it were to his own hindrance:

6 He that hath not given his money upon usury, nor taken reward against the innocent:

7 Whoso doeth these things shall never fall.

¶ *From Trinity Monday to Advent*, Ps. 119, 145–160.

Clamavi in toto corde meo.

I CALL with my whole heart; hear me, O Lord; I will keep thy statutes.

2 Yea, even unto thee do I call; help me, and I shall keep thy testimonies.

3 Early in the morning do I cry unto thee; for in thy word is my trust.

4 Mine eyes prevent the night watches; that I might be occupied in thy words.

5 Hear my voice, O Lord, according unto thy loving-kindness; quicken me, according as thou art wont.

6 They draw nigh that of

malice persecute me, and are far from thy law.

7 Be thou nigh at hand, O Lord; for all thy commandments are true.

8 As concerning thy testimonies, I have known long since, that thou hast grounded them for ever.

Vide humilitatem.

O CONSIDER mine adversity, and deliver me, for I do not forget thy law.

2 Avenge thou my cause, and deliver me; quicken me according to thy word.

3 Health is far from the ungodly; for they regard not thy statutes.

4 Great is thy mercy, O Lord; quicken me, as thou art wont.

5 Many there are that trouble me, and persecute me; yet do I not swerve from thy testimonies.

6 It grieveth me when I see the transgressors; because they keep not thy law.

7 Consider, O Lord, how I love thy commandments; O quicken me, according to thy loving-kindness.

8 Thy word is true from everlasting; all the judgments of thy righteousness endure for evermore.

AT VESPERS.

Psalms 132; 147, 12-20.

PSALM CXXXII. *Memento, Domine.*

LORD, remember David, and all his trouble.

2 How he sware unto the Lord, and vowed a vow unto the Almighty God of Jacob:

3 I will not come within the tabernacle of mine house, nor climb up into my bed;

4 I will not suffer mine eyes to sleep, nor mine eyelids to slumber; neither the temples of my head to take any rest;

5 Until I find out a place for the temple of the Lord; a habitation for the mighty God of Jacob.

6 Lo, we heard of the same at Ephrata, and found it in the wood.

7 We will go into his tabernacle, and fall low on our knees before his footstool.

8 Arise, O Lord, into thy resting-place; thou, and the ark of thy strength.

9 Let thy priests be clothed with righteousness; and let thy saints sing with joyfulness.

10 For thy servant David's sake, turn not away the presence of thine anointed.

11 The Lord hath made a faithful oath unto David, and he shall not shrink from it;

12 Of the fruit of thy body shall I set upon thy seat.

13 If thy children will keep my covenant, and my testimonies that I shall learn them; their children also shall sit upon thy seat for evermore.

14 For the Lord hath chosen Sion to be a habitation for himself: he hath longed for her.

15 This shall be my rest for ever: here will I dwell, for I have a delight therein.

16 I will bless her victuals with increase, and will satisfy her poor with bread.

17 I will deck her priests with health, and her saints shall rejoice and sing.

18 There shall I make the horn of David to flourish: I have ordained a lantern for mine anointed.

19 As for his enemies, I shall clothe them with shame; but upon himself shall his crown flourish.

PSALM cxlvii. 12–20. *Lauda Hierusalem.*

PRAISE the Lord, O Jerusalem; praise thy God, O Sion;
13 For he hath made fast the bars of thy gates, and hath blessed thy children within thee.
14 He maketh peace in thy borders, and filleth thee with the flour of wheat.
15 He sendeth forth his commandment upon earth, and his word runneth very swiftly.
16 He giveth snow like wool, and scattereth the hoar-frost like ashes.
17 He casteth forth his ice like morsels; who is able to abide his frost?
18 He sendeth out his word, and melteth them; he bloweth with his wind, and the waters flow.
19 He showeth his word unto Jacob, his statutes and ordinances unto Israel.
20 He hath not dealt so with any nation; neither have the heathen knowledge of his laws.

IV.

LITANIES, PRAYERS, AND COLLECTS.

LITANIES.

¶ *The following Litanies may be added to the Mutin and Vesper offices at certain Seasons, or on certain Holy Days, or may be recited as substitutes for the offices of the 3d, 6th, and 9th hours, or any one of them at discretion.*

Litany of the Blessed Trinity, on Sundays and during Trinity Season.
Litany of our Blessed Saviour, in Epiphany Season.
Litany of the Most Precious Name, on Circumcision and August 7.
Litany of the Holy Spirit, Whitsuntide; or at the 3d hour of the day.
Litany of the Passion, on Fridays and during Lent; or at the 6th hour.
Litany of the Resurrection, in Easter Tide.
Litany of Penitence, on Ember and Rogation Days, and on Fasts and Days of Abstinence.
Litany of Christian Virtues, Lent, and Trinity Season.

I. Litany of the Blessed Trinity.

LORD, have mercy.

O Holy Unity, of incomprehensible majesty, infinite wisdom, and inexhaustible goodness,
O Eternal Verity, True and only Trinity, one Supreme Deity, of equal power and co-eternal Majesty,
Father unbegotten,
Only begotten Son,
Holy Ghost, from both proceeding,
O Father, our Creator,
O Son, our Redeemer,
O Holy Ghost, our Sanctifier and Comforter,
Father of mercies and God of all consolation,
Father of our Lord Jesus Christ,
Father who hast chosen us in Thy Son before the foundation of the world,
Spirit of Wisdom, of Counsel, and of all Virtues,

} *Have mercy upon us.*

Be merciful, spare us, O Holy Trinity.
Be merciful, hear us, O Holy Trinity.

From all evil and sin,
From all pride and obstinacy,
From all avarice and cov-

} *Holy*

LITANIES.

From everlasting condemnation,
By the power of Thy Omnipotence,
By the Majesty of Thy Glory,
By the multitude of Thy mercies,
By the abundance of Thy clemency,
By the greatness of Thy love,
By the depth of Thy judgments,
By the height of Thy wisdom,
By the riches of Thy blessedness,
In the day of judgment,

} *Holy Trinity, deliver us.*

We sinners beseech Thee to hear us.

That we may worship Thee, our Lord God, and serve Thee only,
That we take not Thy Holy Name in vain,
That we may duly observe and sanctify the Fasts and Feasts of Thy Church,
That we may honour and obey our parents and superiors,
That we hurt nobody by word or deed,
That we commit no uncleanness of mind or body,
That we neither defraud nor do injustice to any,
That we never speak falsely against our neighbours,
That we never covet oth-

} *We beseech Thee to hear us.*

That Thou wouldst bring us to behold Thy Glory,
God the Father, God the Son, and God the Holy Ghost,
Holy, Holy, Holy Lord God of Sabaoth,

} *We beseech Thee to hear us.*

Lamb of God, who takest away the sins of the world,
Render thy Father merciful to us.
Lamb of God, who takest away the sins of the world,
Be Thou merciful unto us.
Lamb of God, who takest away the sins of the world,
Give us thy Holy Spirit.

O blessed Trinity, hear us,
O adorable Unity, hear us.
Lord, have mercy.
Christ, have mercy.
Lord, have mercy.
Our Father, &c.

℣. Blessed art Thou, O Lord God of our Fathers.
℟. Worthy to be praised and glorious for ever.
℣. Blessed art Thou, O Lord in the firmament of heaven.
℟. Worthy to be praised, glorious, and highly exalted for ever.
℣. Let all Thy angels and Saints bless Thee.
℟. Praise Thee and glorify Thee for ever.
℣. Bless we the Father and the Son with the Holy Ghost.
℟. Praise we and magnify Him for ever.
℣. O Lord, hear my prayer.
℟. And let my cry come unto Thee.

in us profound humility and constant obedience, and the frequent meditation of Thy infinite goodness may make us to love Thee above all things, that we may here stedfastly believe what we do not see, and hereafter, in the blessed vision of Thy glory, see what we now cannot comprehend, through Jesus Christ our Lord, who, with Thee and the Holy Ghost, liveth and reigneth, one God, for ever and ever. *Amen.*

II. LITANY OF OUR BLESSED SAVIOUR.

LORD, have mercy on us.
 Christ, have mercy on us.
 Lord, have mercy on us.
 Jesus, receive our prayers.
 Lord Jesus, grant our petitions.

O God the Father, Creator of the world,
 O God the Son, Redeemer of mankind,
 O God the Holy Ghost, Perfecter of the elect,
 Holy Trinity, one God,
 Jesus, Son of the living God,
 Jesus, the express image of Thy Father's glory,
 Jesus, the bright ray of eternal light,
 Jesus, the uncreated wisdom, by whom all things are governed,
 Jesus, the eternal word, made man for our redemption,
 Jesus, most blessed Son of the Virgin Mary,
 Jesus, most powerful,
 Jesus, most glorious,
 Jesus, most humble and meek,
 Jesus, most patient and } *Have mercy upon us.*

Jesus, most chaste and holy,
 Jesus, lover of poverty,
 Jesus, lover of peace,
 Jesus, lover of us ungrateful sinners,
 Jesus, who camest down from heaven to teach us with Thy own mouth the truths of salvation,
 Jesus, who didst converse so long on earth, to show us by Thy own holy example the way to heaven,
 Jesus, who didst die, even the death of the Cross, to redeem us, and to take off our aversion from suffering, and teach us to endure all things for everlasting happiness,
 Jesus, who didst ascend into heaven, to confirm our belief, and raise our affections to the true joys of eternity,
 Jesus, author of our faith and finisher of our hope,
 Jesus, supreme object of our love and overflowing satiety of all our desires,
 Jesus, our God, blessed for ever, } *Have mercy upon us.*

Have mercy and spare us, O Jesus.
 Have mercy and hear us, O Jesus.

From all evil, from all sin, and from everlasting death,
 By the mystery of Thy holy Incarnation and humble Nativity,
 By the sanctity of Thy heavenly doctrine and miraculous life,
 By the merits of Thy bitter Passion and all-reviving death, } *Good Lord, deliver us*

rious resurrection and triumphant ascension,

By the glory of Thy eternal kingdom and incomprehensible majesty,

We sinners beseech Thee to hear us.

That it would please Thee to protect and govern Thy Holy Church, which Thou hast purchased with Thy precious Blood,

That looking continually on Thy admirable life we may faithfully endeavour to follow Thy steps,

That denying all vicious and inordinate inclinations we may live soberly, justly, and piously,

That through Thy love the world may be crucified to us, and we to the world,

That whatever we ask in Thy holy Name, we may receive through Thy Infinite merits,

We beseech Thee to hear us.

Son of God, we beseech Thee to hear us.

Lamb of God, who takest away the sins of the world, (*Thrice.*)
 — Spare us, O Jesus.
 Hear us, O Jesus.
 Have mercy on us.

Lord, have mercy on us.
Christ, have mercy on us.
Lord, have mercy on us.
Our Father, &c.

Antiphon. Every day we will repeat Thy perfections, O glorious Jesus! that every day we may grow in our esteem of Thee. Every day we will attentively reckon Thy mercies, that every day we may increase in Thy love.

we received from Thy grace. Alleluia.

℟. All we desire and hope we expect in Thy glory. Alleluia.

℣. O Lord, hear my prayer.

℟. And let my cry come unto Thee.

Let us pray.

ALMIGHTY GOD, and most merciful Saviour, the Light of this world and the glory of the next; vouchsafe, we beseech Thee, to illuminate our understandings, and inflame our wills, and sanctify all the faculties of our souls; that whilst with our lips we recite these prayers, we may inwardly with our hearts adore Thy person, admire Thy goodness, and conform our lives to Thy holy example, till at length, by frequent meditation on the bliss Thou hast prepared for us hereafter, we break off our affections from all irregular adherence to this world, and place them entirely on the enjoyment of Thee, who, with the Father and the Holy Ghost, livest and reignest, one God, world without end. Amen.

May the blessing of God Almighty, Father, Son, and Holy Ghost, descend upon us, and dwell in our hearts for ever. Amen.

III. Litany of the Most Precious Name of Jesus.

LORD, have mercy on us.
Christ, have mercy on us.
Lord, have mercy on us.
O Christ, hear us.
O Christ, listen to our prayers.
O God the Father of Heaven,
O God the Son, Redeemer

LITANIES.

O God the Holy Ghost,
O most Holy Trinity, one eternal God,
O Jesus, Son of the living God,
O Jesus, of all the most mighty,
O Jesus, of all the most glorious,
O Jesus, of all the most powerful,
O Jesus, of all the most perfect,
O Jesus, of all the most merciful, loving and kind,
O Jesus, of all the poorest and meekest,
O Jesus, of all the most patient and condescending,
O Jesus, lover of purity and peace,
O Jesus, lover of chastity, mirror of life, pattern of all virtues,
O Jesus, the desire of our souls and our refuge,
O Jesus, Father of the poor, comforter of the afflicted, treasure of Thy faithful people,
O Jesus, precious stone, source of all perfection,
O Jesus, good shepherd of the sheep,
O Jesus, light of the world, bright and morning star,
O Jesus, wisdom eternal, unsearchable goodness,
O Jesus, joy of the angels,
O Jesus, king of the patriarchs,
O Jesus, leader of the prophets,
O Jesus, master of the apostles,
O Jesus, teacher of the evangelists,
O Jesus, strength of the martyrs,
O Jesus, light of the confessors,
O Jesus, chastity of the virgins, and crown of all saints,
} *Have mercy upon us.*

Be merciful and forgive us,
Be merciful and hearken unto us,
Be merciful unto us and deliver us,
} *O gracious Jesu.*

From all sin, and from Thy wrath,
From sloth, and from sudden death,
From plague, pestilence, and famine,
From the wicked spirit,
From storm and tempest,
From everlasting death,
From transgressing Thy commandments,
From every assault of the devil,
By the mystery of Thy Incarnation,
By the love wherewith Thou didst come down from heaven into the world, by Thy sacred birth,
By the love with which Thou didst endure Thy labours and travails for three and thirty years,
By Thy bitter passion,
By Thy holy cross and agony, innocent as Thou art,
By Thy all-reviving death,
By Thy joys and glory,
By Thy glorious resurrection, and triumphant ascension into heaven,
} *O Lord, deliver us.*

O Lamb of God, that takest away the sins of the world, (*Thrice.*)
} Forgive us, O Jesus. Hear us, O Jesus. Have mercy on us.

Our Father, &c.

The Lord's name be praised;
 Now and for evermore.
Lord, hear our prayer;
 And let our cry come unto Thee.

Prayer.

O GOD, who hast made the glorious name of Jesus Christ Thy Son our Lord most precious and beloved to all believers, but dreadful and terrible to all evil spirits; grant, O merciful Father, that we who honour Thy holy name here on earth, may during this life enjoy the sweetness of Thy holy comforts, and in the life to come, everlasting rest and blessedness; through the same Jesus Christ our Lord. *Amen.*

IV. LITANY OF THE PASSION.

LORD, have mercy upon us.
 Christ, have mercy upon us.
Lord, have mercy upon us.

O God the Father,
O God the Son,
O God, the Holy Ghost,
Holy Trinity, one God,
Jesus, son of the living God, } *Have mercy upon us miserable sinners.*

From all evil,
From sudden, unprepared and evil death,
From the snares of the devil,
From anger, hatred, and ill will,
From everlasting death,
By the mystery of Thy holy incarnation,
By Thy most holy life and conversation,
By Thine agony and bloody sweat,
By Thy thrice repeated prayer,
By the resignation of Thy human will,
By Thy bonds and stripes,
By Thy sacred body, buffeted and smitten,
By Thy cruel mockings and scourgings,
By the spitting upon Thine adorable face,
By the false judgment pronounced on Thee by Caiphas,
By Thy being set at naught by Herod,
By the shameful stripping off of Thy garments,
By Thy painful crown of thorns,
By Thy purple robe of mockery,
By Thy unjust condemnation,
By Thy bearing Thine own cross,
By Thy footprints traced in blood,
By the tearing off of Thy garments,
By the cruel straining of Thy sacred limbs,
By Thy dread crucifixion,
By the upraising of Thy cross,
By the anguish which Thou didst suffer,
By the insults which Thou didst endure,
By Thy prayers and tears,
By the shedding of Thy precious blood,
By Thy patience and humility,
By Thy seven precious sayings on the cross,
By the love wherewith Thou didst love us even unto the end, } *Good Lord, deliver us.*

LITANIES.

We sinners do beseech Thee, O Jesu, to hear us.

That being dead unto sin, we may live unto righteousness,

That we glory not, save in Thy cross, O Lord Jesus Christ,

That we take up our cross daily and follow Thee,

That Thy blood may cleanse us from dead works to serve the living God,

That, looking unto Thy example, we may follow Thy steps,

That being partakers of Thy sufferings, we may be also of Thy glory,

} *We beseech Thee to hear us.*

Lamb of God that takest away the sin of the world, (*Thrice.*)
Spare us, good Lord.
Hear us, good Lord.
Have mercy upon us.

O Saviour of the world, who through Thy cross and precious blood hast redeemed us, save us and help us we humbly beseech Thee, O Lord.

℣. We adore Thee, O Jesus, and bless Thee.

℟. Because by Thy cross and passion Thou hast redeemed the world.

℣. Remember, O Lord, Thy tender mercies.

℟. And Thy loving-kindnesses which have been ever of old.

℣. Look upon mine adversity and misery.

℟. And forgive me all my sin.

℣. Lord, hear our prayer.

℟. And let our cry come unto Thee.

Let us pray.

Our Father, &c.

O LORD Jesus Christ, Son of the living God, who, at the sixth hour, wast lifted up upon the cross for the redemption of the world, and didst shed Thy blood for the remission of our sins; we humbly beseech Thee, that by the virtue and merits of Thy most holy life, passion, and death, Thou wouldest grant us to enter into the gates of Paradise with joy. Who livest and reignest one God, world without end. *Amen.*

V. LITANY OF THE RESURRECTION.

LORD, have mercy.
Christ, have mercy.
Lord, have mercy.

O God, the Father of Heaven,

O God, the Son, Redeemer of the world,

O God, the Holy Ghost, Sanctifier of the faithful,

O Holy Trinity, one God,

O Lord Jesus Christ, the true Paschal Lamb,

Jesus, who didst build up in three days the temple of Thy body,

Jesus, who according to Thy word didst rise the third day from Thy grave,

Jesus, whose resurrection an angel announced to the women at the sepulchre,

Jesus, who didst show Thyself to Thy disciples after Thy resurrection,

Jesus, who didst manifest the truth of Thy resurrection with unnumbered miracles,

Jesus, whose resurrection the Apostles preached and confirmed with their blood,

} *Have mercy upon us miserable sinners.*

LITANIES.

Jesus, who through Thy resurrection hast given us a sure hope of eternal life,
Jesus, who after Thy resurrection didst continue forty days with Thy disciples,
Jesus, who didst ascend from the mount of Olives to Thy Father and ours,
Jesus, who hast prepared mansions in Thy Father's house for Thy servants,
Jesus, who wilt come again to judge both the quick and the dead,

} *Have mercy upon us miserable sinners.*

We, sinners, beseech Thee to hear us,
That we may truly rise from the grave of our sins,
That we may conquer our evil desires and die to our sins,
That we may grow in knowledge and love of Thy holy teaching,
That we may serve Thee in holiness and righteousness all the days of our life,
That our sorrows, like Thine, may one day be turned into eternal joy,
That we may not seek after things on earth but things in heaven,
That we may awake at length from the grave to the resurrection of eternal life,
That at the general resurrection we may have a share in Thy kingdom,
Son of God, we beseech Thee to hear us.

Lord, have mercy upon us.
Christ, have mercy upon us.
Lord, have mercy upon us.

Our Father, &c.

℣. Lighten mine eyes, O Lord.
℟. That I sleep not in death.

℣. Help me now, O Lord.
℟. O Lord, send us now prosperity.

Let us pray.

O MERCIFUL SAVIOUR, make us partakers of the comfort of Thy holy resurrection and ascension, that being supported with Thy heavenly grace in this life, we may hereafter ascend to Thee, and appearing before Thy glorious judgment-seat pure and unspotted, may receive a happy place, and sing Thy praises for ever, who livest and reignest with the Father and the Holy Ghost, world without end. Amen.

VI. LITANY OF THE HOLY SPIRIT.

LORD, have mercy on us.
Christ, have mercy on us.
Lord, have mercy on us.

Holy Spirit, proceeding from the Father and the Son,
Spirit of the Lord God of Israel,
Holy Spirit, author of all good,
Holy Spirit, by whose inspiration holy men formerly spake,
Holy Spirit, who didst overshadow the blessed Virgin Mary, by whose mysterious energy the Incarnation of our Lord was wrought in her womb,
Spirit of truth, teaching and guiding us into all truth,
Spirit of wisdom and understanding,
Spirit of counsel and might, of knowledge and piety,
Spirit of prudence and of the fear of the Lord, gift and promise of the Father

} *Have mercy upon us.*

and the Son, who didst descend to abide with and dwell in us,

Holy Spirit, the Paraclete, reproving the world, our Advocate and Intercessor here on earth,

Holy Spirit, by whom we are regenerate and made sons of God,

Holy Spirit, by whom the love of God is shed abroad in our hearts,

Spirit of adoption, by whom we cry Abba Father,

Spirit of grace and compassion, bearing witness with our spirits that we are the sons of God,

Spirit of sweetness and benignity, the pledge of our heavenly inheritance, leading us in the right way,

Holy Spirit, the bond of the mystical union between Christ our head and us his members,

O Holy Ghost, the Comforter, in all afflictions, giving us strength to bear them, and inward peace and joy under them. *Have mercy upon us.*

O Spirit of all graces, dividing Thy sevenfold gifts to every man according to Thy will. *Have mercy upon us.*

Be favourable and spare us, O Holy Spirit.

Be favourable and hear us, O Holy Spirit.

Spirit of the Living God. *Deliver us.*

From the spirit of error,

From fornication and the spirit of uncleanness,

From the spirit of blasphemy and from all deceits of the devil,

From all obstinacy and desperation,

From all presumption and contradiction of the truth,

From all anger, malice, and envy, and from evil habits,

From all hatred and want of brotherly charity,

From hardness of heart and final impenitence,

By Thy eternal procession from the Father and the Son,

By Thy mighty working in the miraculous conception of the Son of God in the Virgin's womb,

By Thy descent upon Him at his baptism,

By Thy descent in fiery tongues upon the apostles on the day of Pentecost, and by all Thy mighty acts through them,

By Thy ineffable goodness by which Thou dost govern Thy church, preside in councils, strengthen martyrs, illuminate doctors, and institute and replenish religious orders.

We sinners beseech Thee to hear us,

That we may walk in the Spirit and not fulfil the lusts of the flesh,

That Thou wouldst inspire us with a hatred of sin and write Thy laws on our hearts,

That Thou wouldst kindle in us the fire of Thy love and teach us to love one another,

That Thou wouldst give to all Christian people one heart and one spirit,

That Thou wouldst vouchsafe to fill us with all virtues,

That Thou wouldst enlighten us and make us obedient to Thy holy Inspirations,

That Thou wouldst vouchsafe to keep the bishops and clergy in Thy true religion,

That Thou wouldst endue us with the grace of final perseverance,

O Spirit of God, &c.

O Lamb of God, who takest away the sins of the world, Pour Thy Holy Spirit upon us.

O Lamb of God, who takest, &c. Send down upon us the Spirit promised of the Father.

O Lamb of God, &c. Grant us Thy good Spirit.

Our Father, &c.

℣. Make me a clean heart, O God.

℟. And renew a right spirit within me.

℣. Cast me not away from Thy presence.

℟. And take not Thy Holy Spirit from me.

℣. O give me the comfort of Thy help again.

℟. And stablish me with Thy free Spirit.

℣. Lord, hear my prayer.

℟. And let my cry come unto Thee.

O HEAVENLY KING, Thou Comforter and Spirit of Truth, who art in every place and fillest the whole world with the treasures of Thy goodness, O Lord, O Life-Giver, come into our hearts, and dwell there, and save our souls alive, and to Thee, one with the Father and the Son, be glory, now and evermore. Amen.

LITANIES.

VII. LITANY OF CHRISTIAN VIRTUES.

O God the Father of heaven,
O God the Son, Redeemer of the world,
O God the Holy Ghost, sanctifier of the elect,
O blessed and glorious Trinity, one God,
O Lord, just and good, the rewarder of all them that diligently seek Thee,
O God, who didst create our first parents in Thine own image, in innocence and holiness, and didst accept the offering of righteous Abel, savedst Noah from the flood, and just Lot from the destruction of Sodom,
Thou who didst give the promise to faithful Abraham, deliveredst Jacob, and gavest a prosperous end to patient Job,
Who didst reward the chastity and meekness of Joseph with rule over Egypt, and chosest the meek Moses to rule over Thy people, and faithful Joshua to lead them to the promised land,
Who gavest the priesthood to the sons of Levi, for their zeal and courage in avenging Thine honour, and deliveredst the zealous Elijah from all his troubles, by taking him up to heaven,
Who didst set Samuel, a lover of justice and hater of bribes, to judge Thy people.
Who didst exalt David, the man after Thine own heart, to the throne of Israel, and adorn Solomon

Have mercy upon us.

with wondrous wisdom and many other gifts,
Who didst adorn the temperate and holy Daniel with wisdom, abstinence, and beauty,
Who didst choose the blessed Virgin Mary, adorned with chastity, humility, and obedience, to be the mother of Thy Son,
Who didst send Thine only-begotten Son into the world to be the pattern of all holiness, that we should follow his example,
Who hast delivered us from darkness into marvellous light, and from the power of Satan unto Thyself, and hast given us remission of sins and inheritance among Thy saints,

Have mercy upon us.

Be merciful and help us, O Lord.

Be merciful and grant unto us, O Lord, the graces of humility and poverty of spirit, meekness, long-suffering, and obedience to those set over us.

A quiet and thankful mind, contented with our condition in life, true peace and joy in the Holy Ghost,

Grant unto us, O Lord.

Temperance and modesty, sobriety and chastity, true love of Thee and of our neighbours, a humble opinion of ourselves and the things of this world, bounty and compassion towards others,

Grant unto us, O Lord.

Diligence and watchfulness, hungering and thirsting after holiness, zeal, and fervour of spirit in Thy cause, and Christian fortitude and patience unto the end,

Grant unto us, O Lord.

PART II.

We, sinners, beseech Thee to hear us,

That, being reconciled to Thee by the death of Thy Son, we may be presented holy, unspotted, and unblamable before Thee, that we may walk worthy of our Christian calling, being faithful in every good word and work, increasing in the knowledge of God,

That whatsoever we do in word or deed we may do all to Thy glory, and not receive Thy grace in vain,

That we may always sanctify the Lord God in our hearts, and seek not our own, but the things of Christ's,

That looking up to Jesus, who suffered for us, we be not weary and faint in our minds, but considering his example and the conversations of the saints, may imitate their faith and patience,

That as the soldiers and baptized servants of Christ, we may not entangle ourselves unduly in the affairs of this life, but having food and raiment be therewith content,

That we may forbear one another in love, striving to keep the unity of the Spirit in the bond of peace; that bearing one another's burdens we may fulfil the law of Christ; that being strengthened in all virtue through the power of Thy grace, we may give thanks to Thee for all things,

That, waiting for the coming of our Lord Jesus Christ, we may be found in

We beseech Thee to hear us, O Lord.

Him pure and unspotted, that we may receive the end of our faith, even the salvation of our souls,

O Lamb of God, that takest away the sins of the world, (*Thrice.*) } *Increase our faith. Confirm our hope. Kindle our charity.*

O Christ, hear us.
Lord, have mercy, &c.
Christ, have mercy, &c.
Lord, have mercy, &c.
Our Father, &c.

O GOD, who makest all things to work together for good to them that love Thee, pour into our hearts such steadfast love to Thee, that our longings, which by Thy inspiration we conceive, may not be turned aside by any temptation. Inflame, O Lord, our hearts with the fire of Thy Holy Spirit, that we may serve Thee with a chaste body and please Thee with a clean heart. *Amen.*

O GOD, who by the endurance of Thy only-begotten hast bruised the pride of the old enemy; grant to us, we beseech Thee, worthily to call to mind what He lovingly endured for us; so that by his example we may patiently bear our adversities. We humbly beseech Thee graciously to protect with Thy heavenly aid us Thy servants who lean only on Thy mercy, and to keep us with Thy continual defence; that no temptation may ever separate us from Thee, but that running unwearied the race of virtue, we may at length receive the prize, through our Lord Jesus Christ. *Amen.*

VIII. LITANY OF PENITENCE.

Lord, have mercy upon us.
Christ, have mercy upon us.
Lord, have mercy upon us.
O God the Father, &c.
O God the Son, &c.
O God the Holy Ghost, &c.
Holy Trinity one God,
O God who wouldest not the death of a sinner, but rather that he should be converted and live,
Who sparedst not the angels that sinned, but didst cast them down to hell,
Who calledst Adam, after his fall, to penitence and acknowledgment of his sin,
Who didst fearfully punish Pharaoh, feigning repentance yet hardened in heart,
Who forgavest Thy disobedient people at the prayer of Moses,
Who forgavest the Amorites, repenting in sackcloth and ashes,
Who by Thy prophet Nathan broughtest David to a sense of sin,
Who didst put away his sin when he humbly confessed it,
Who sparedst Ahab when he humbled himself before Thee,
Who camest into the world to save sinners,
Who broughtest salvation to the house of Zaccheus when he restored fourfold,
Who mercifully heardest the Canaanitish woman when she persevered in prayer,
Who receivedst publicans and sinners, and didst eat with them,

} *Have mercy upon us.*

LITANIES.

Who freely forgavest the sins of Mary Magdalene who loved much,
Who in mercy lookedst upon Peter, who denied Thee, moving him to confess his sin and to shed tears of penitence,
Who on the cross didst promise Paradise to the penitent thief,
Who Thyself didst no sin, and yet didst bear our sins in Thy body on the tree,
Who wast bruised for our transgressions, and wounded for our iniquities,
Who wouldest not that any should perish, but that all should come to repentance,
Who camest to seek and to save that which was lost,
Who after our repentance rememberest our sins no more,
} *Have mercy upon us.*

Be merciful and spare us, good Lord.

From all evil and wickedness,
From sudden, unprepared, or evil death,
By Thy blood which Thou didst shed for the remission of our sins,
In time of trouble, in the hour of death, and in the day of judgment,
} *Good Lord, deliver us.*

We sinners do beseech Thee to hear us.

That it may please Thee to bring us to true repentance,
That, condemning ourselves, we may escape Thy condemnation,
That we may bring forth worthy fruits of penitence,
That we give not place to the devil, nor let the sun go down upon our wrath,
That, denying ungodliness and worldly lusts, we may live soberly, righteously, and godly in this present world,
That, being dead unto sin, we may live unto righteousness,
That we may work out our salvation with fear and trembling,
That, coming boldly to the throne of grace, we may find grace to help in time of need,
} *␣␣␣␣␣␣␣␣␣␣Thee to hear us, good Lord.*

O Lamb of God, that takest away the sins of the world, (*Thrice.*) } Spare us, O Lord.
Hear us, O Lord.
Have mercy upon us.

Our Father, &c.

℣. O Lord, deal not with us after our sins.

℟. Neither reward us after our iniquities.

℣. O Lord, remember not our old sins.

℟. But have mercy upon us and that soon, for we are brought very low.

℣. Help us, O God our Saviour.

℟. And for the glory of Thy name deliver us and be merciful unto our sins for Thy Name's sake.

℣. Cleanse us, O Lord, from our secret faults.

℟. And keep Thy servants from presumptuous sins.

℣. Lord, hear my prayer.

℟. And let my cry come unto Thee.

119

LITANIES.

Let us pray.

O LORD Jesus Christ, Saviour of the world, who gavest Thyself to death upon the cross to save sinners, have mercy upon us, and be not angry with us for ever. Accept our contrition, pardon our offences, hear our prayers, that, freed from the bondage of our sins, we may evermore cleave unto Thee in this life, and finally be received by Thee unto life eternal. *Amen.*

COLLECTS AND PRAYERS.

The First Sunday in Advent.

ALMIGHTY God, give us grace that we may cast away the works of darkness, and put upon us the armour of light, now in the time of this mortal life, in which Thy Son Jesus Christ came to visit us in great humility; that in the last day, when He shall come again in his glorious Majesty to judge both the quick and dead, we may rise to the life immortal, through Him who liveth and reigneth with Thee and the Holy Ghost, now and ever. *Amen.*

The Second Sunday in Advent.

BLESSED Lord, who hast caused all holy Scriptures to be written for our learning; Grant that we may in such wise hear them, read, mark, learn, and inwardly digest them, that by patience, and comfort of Thy holy Word, we may embrace, and ever hold fast the blessed hope of everlasting life, which Thou hast given us in our Saviour Jesus Christ. *Amen.*

Third Sunday in Advent.

O LORD Jesus Christ, who at Thy first coming didst send Thy messenger to prepare Thy way before Thee; Grant that the ministers and stewards of Thy mysteries may likewise so prepare and make ready Thy way, by turning the hearts of the disobedient to the wisdom of the just, that at Thy second coming to judge the world we may be found an acceptable people in Thy sight, who livest and reignest with the Father and the Holy Spirit, ever one God, world without end. *Amen.*

The Fourth Sunday in Advent.

O LORD, raise up, we pray Thee, Thy power, and come among us, and with great might succour us; that whereas, through our sins and wickedness, we are sore let and hindered in running the race that is set before us, Thy bountiful grace and mercy may speedily help and deliver us; through the satisfaction of Thy Son our Lord, to whom, with Thee and the Holy Ghost, be honour and glory, world without end. *Amen.*

The Nativity of our Lord, or the Birth-day of Christ, commonly called Christmas-day.

ALMIGHTY God, who hast given us Thy only-begotten Son to take our nature upon Him, and as at this time to be born of a pure virgin; Grant that we being regenerate, and made Thy children by adoption and grace, may daily be renewed

COLLECTS AND PRAYERS.

by Thy Holy Spirit; through the same our Lord Jesus Christ, who liveth and reigneth with Thee and the same Spirit, ever one God, world without end. *Amen.*

The Circumcision of Christ.

ALMIGHTY God, who madest Thy blessed Son to be circumcised, and obedient to the Law for man; Grant us the true Circumcision of the Spirit; that, our hearts, and all our members, being mortified from all worldly and carnal lusts, we may in all things obey Thy blessed will; through the same Thy Son Jesus Christ our Lord. *Amen.*

The Epiphany, or the Manifestation of Christ to the Gentiles.

O GOD, who by the leading of a star didst manifest Thy only-begotten Son to the Gentiles; Mercifully grant that we, who know Thee now by faith, may after this life have the fruition of Thy glorious Godhead; through Jesus Christ our Lord. *Amen.*

The First Sunday after the Epiphany.

O LORD, we beseech Thee mercifully to receive the prayers of Thy people who call upon Thee; and grant that they may both perceive and know what things they ought to do, and also may have grace and power faithfully to fulfil the same; through Jesus Christ our Lord. *Amen.*

The Second Sunday after the Epiphany.

ALMIGHTY and everlasting God, who dost govern all things in heaven and earth; Mercifully hear the supplications of Thy people, and grant us Thy peace all the days of our life; through Jesus Christ our Lord. *Amen.*

The Third Sunday after the Epiphany.

ALMIGHTY and everlasting God, mercifully look upon our infirmities, and in all our dangers and necessities stretch forth Thy right hand to help and defend us; through Jesus Christ our Lord. *Amen.*

The Fourth Sunday after the Epiphany.

O GOD, who knowest us to be set in the midst of so many and great dangers, that by reason of the frailty of our nature we cannot always stand upright; Grant to us such strength and protection, as may support us in all dangers, and carry us through all temptations; through Jesus Christ our Lord. *Amen.*

The Fifth Sunday after the Epiphany.

O LORD, we beseech Thee to keep Thy Church and household continually in Thy true religion; that they who do lean only upon the hope of Thy heavenly grace may evermore be defended by Thy mighty power; through Jesus Christ our Lord. *Amen.*

The Sixth Sunday after the Epiphany.

O GOD, whose blessed Son was manifested that He might destroy the works of the devil, and make us the sons of God, and heirs of eternal life; Grant us, we beseech Thee, that, having this hope, we may purify ourselves even as He is pure;

that, when He shall appear again with power and great glory, we may be made like unto Him in his eternal and glorious kingdom; where with Thee, O Father, and Thee, O Holy Ghost, He liveth and reigneth, ever one God, world without end. *Amen.*

The Sunday called Septuagesima, or the Third Sunday before Lent.

O LORD, we beseech Thee favourably to hear the prayers of Thy people; that we, who are justly punished for our offences, may be mercifully delivered by Thy goodness, for the glory of Thy Name; through Jesus Christ our Saviour, who liveth and reigneth with Thee and the Holy Ghost, ever one God, world without end. *Amen.*

The Sunday called Sexagesima, or the Second Sunday before Lent.

O LORD God, who seest that we put not our trust in any thing that we do; Mercifully grant that by Thy power we may be defended against all adversity; through Jesus Christ our Lord. *Amen.*

The Sunday called Quinquagesima, or the next Sunday before Lent.

O LORD, who hast taught us that all our doings without charity are nothing worth; Send Thy Holy Ghost, and pour into our hearts that most excellent gift of charity, the very bond of peace and of all virtues, without which whosoever liveth is counted dead before Thee. Grant this for Thine only Son Jesus Christ's sake. *Amen.*

that Thou hast made, and dost forgive the sins of all those who are penitent; Create and make in us new and contrite hearts, that we worthily lamenting our sins, and acknowledging our wretchedness, may obtain of Thee, the God of all mercy, perfect remission and forgiveness; through Jesus Christ our Lord. *Amen.*

The First Sunday in Lent.

O LORD, who for our sake didst fast forty days and forty nights; Give us grace to use such abstinence, that, our flesh being subdued to the Spirit, we may ever obey Thy godly motions in righteousness, and true holiness, to Thy honour and glory, who livest and reignest with the Father and the Holy Ghost, one God, world without end. *Amen.*

The Second Sunday in Lent.

ALMIGHTY God, who seest that we have no power of ourselves to help ourselves; Keep us both outwardly in our bodies, and inwardly in our souls; that we may be defended from all adversities which may happen to the body, and from all evil thoughts which may assault and hurt the soul; through Jesus Christ our Lord. *Amen.*

The Third Sunday in Lent.

WE beseech Thee, Almighty God, look upon the hearty desires of thy humble servants, and stretch forth the right hand of Thy Majesty, to be our defence against all our enemies; through Jesus Christ our Lord. *Amen.*

who for our evil deeds do worthily deserve to be punished, by the comfort of Thy grace may mercifully be relieved; through our Lord and Saviour Jesus Christ. *Amen.*

The Fifth Sunday in Lent.

WE beseech Thee, Almighty God, mercifully to look upon Thy people; that by Thy great goodness they may be governed and preserved evermore, both in body and soul; through Jesus Christ our Lord. *Amen.*

The Sunday next before Easter.

ALMIGHTY and everlasting God, who, of Thy tender love towards mankind, hast sent Thy Son, our Saviour Jesus Christ, to take upon Him our flesh, and to suffer death upon the cross, that all mankind should follow the example of his great humility; Mercifully grant, that we may both follow the example of His patience, and also be made partakers of His resurrection; through the same Jesus Christ our Lord. *Amen.*

Good Friday.

ALMIGHTY God, we beseech Thee graciously to behold this Thy family, for which our Lord Jesus Christ was contented to be betrayed, and given up into the hands of wicked men, and to suffer death upon the cross, who now liveth and reigneth with Thee and the Holy Ghost, ever one God, world without end. *Amen.*

ALMIGHTY and everlasting God, by whose Spirit the whole body of the Church is governed and sanctified; Receive our supplications and prayers, which we offer before Thee for all estates of men in Thy holy Church, that every member of the same, in his vocation and ministry, may truly and godly serve Thee; through our Lord and Saviour Jesus Christ. *Amen.*

O MERCIFUL God, who hast made all men, and hatest nothing that Thou hast made, nor desirest the death of a sinner, but rather that he should be converted and live; Have mercy upon all Jews, Turks, Infidels, and Heretics; and take from them all ignorance, hardness of heart, and contempt of Thy Word; and so fetch them home, blessed Lord, to Thy flock, that they may be saved among the remnant of the true Israelites, and be made one fold under one shepherd, Jesus Christ our Lord, who liveth and reigneth with Thee and the Holy Spirit, one God, world without end. *Amen.*

Easter-Even.

GRANT, O Lord, that as we are baptized into the death of Thy blessed Son our Saviour Jesus Christ, so by continual mortifying our corrupt affections we may be buried with him; and that through the grave, and gate of death, we may pass to our joyful resurrection; for His merits who died, and was buried, and rose again for us, thy Son Jesus Christ our Lord. *Amen.*

Easter-Day.

ALMIGHTY God, who through Thine only-begotten Son Jesus Christ hast overcome death and opened unto us the gate of everlasting life; We humbly beseech Thee, that, as by thy special grace preventing us Thou dost put into our minds good desires, so by Thy continual help we may bring the same to good effect; through Jesus Christ our Lord, who liveth and reigneth with Thee and the Holy Ghost, ever one God, world without end. *Amen.*

The First Sunday after Easter.

ALMIGHTY Father, who hast given Thine only Son to die for our sins, and to rise again for our justification; Grant us so to put away the leaven of malice and wickedness, that we may always serve Thee in pureness of living and truth; through the merits of the same Thy Son Jesus Christ our Lord. *Amen.*

The Second Sunday after Easter.

ALMIGHTY God, who hast given Thine only Son to be unto us both a sacrifice for sin, and also an ensample of godly life; Give us grace that we may always most thankfully receive that His inestimable benefit, and also daily endeavour ourselves to follow the blessed steps of His most holy life; through the same Jesus Christ our Lord. *Amen.*

The Third Sunday after Easter.

ALMIGHTY God, who showest to them that are in error the light of Thy truth, to the intent that they may return into the way of righteousness; Grant unto all those who are admitted into the fellowship of Christ's religion, that they may avoid those things that are contrary to their profession, and follow all such things as are agreeable to the same; through our Lord Jesus Christ. *Amen.*

The Fourth Sunday after Easter.

O ALMIGHTY God, who alone canst order the unruly wills and affections of sinful men; Grant unto Thy people, that they may love the thing which Thou commandest, and desire that which Thou dost promise; that so, among the sundry and manifold changes of the world, our hearts may surely there be fixed, where true joys are to be found; through Jesus Christ our Lord. *Amen.*

The Fifth Sunday after Easter.

O LORD, from whom all good things do come, Grant to us Thy humble servants, that by Thy holy inspiration we may think those things that are good, and by Thy merciful guiding may perform the same; through our Lord Jesus Christ. *Amen.*

The Ascension-day.

GRANT, we beseech thee, Almighty God, that like as we do believe Thy only-begotten Son our Lord Jesus Christ to have ascended into the heavens; so we may also in heart and mind thither ascend, and with Him continually dwell, who liveth and reigneth with thee and the Holy Ghost, one God, world without end. *Amen.*

Sunday after Ascension-day.

O GOD the King of glory, who hast exalted Thine only Son Jesus Christ with great triumph unto Thy kingdom in heaven; We beseech Thee, leave us not comfortless; but send to us Thine Holy Ghost to comfort us, and exalt us unto the same place whither our Saviour Christ is gone before, who liveth and reigneth with Thee and the Holy Ghost, one God, world without end. *Amen.*

Whitsunday.

O GOD, who as at this time didst teach the hearts of Thy faithful people, by sending to them the light of Thy Holy Spirit; Grant us by the same Spirit to have a right judgment in all things, and evermore to rejoice in His holy comfort; through the merits of Christ Jesus our Saviour, who liveth and reigneth with Thee, in the unity of the same Spirit, one God, world without end. *Amen.*

Trinity-Sunday.

ALMIGHTY and everlasting God, who hast given unto us Thy servants grace, by the confession of a true faith, to acknowledge the glory of the eternal Trinity, and in the power of the Divine Majesty to worship the Unity; We beseech Thee that Thou wouldest keep us steadfast in this faith, and evermore defend us from all adversities, who livest and reignest, one God, world without end. *Amen.*

The first Sunday after Trinity.

O GOD, the strength of all those who put their trust in Thee; Mercifully accept our prayers: and because, through the weakness of our mortal nature, we can do no good thing without Thee, grant us the help of Thy grace, that in keeping Thy commandments we may please Thee, both in will and deed; through Jesus Christ our Lord. *Amen.*

The Second Sunday after Trinity.

O LORD, who never failest to help and govern those whom Thou dost bring up in Thy steadfast fear and love; Keep us, we beseech Thee, under the protection of Thy good providence, and make us to have a perpetual fear and love of Thy holy Name; through Jesus Christ our Lord. *Amen.*

The Third Sunday after Trinity.

O LORD, we beseech Thee mercifully to hear us; and grant that we, to whom Thou hast given an hearty desire to pray, may, by Thy mighty aid, be defended and comforted in all dangers and adversities; through Jesus Christ our Lord. *Amen.*

The Fourth Sunday after Trinity.

O GOD, the protector of all that trust in Thee, without whom nothing is strong, nothing is holy; increase and multiply upon us Thy mercy; that, Thou being our ruler and guide, we may so pass through things temporal, that we finally lose not the things eternal. Grant this, O heavenly Father, for Jesus Christ's sake our Lord. *Amen.*

The Fifth Sunday after Trinity.

GRANT, O Lord, we beseech Thee, that the course of this world may be so peaceably ordered by Thy governance, that Thy Church may joyfully serve Thee in all godly quietness; through Jesus Christ our Lord. *Amen.*

The Sixth Sunday after Trinity.

O GOD, who hast prepared for those who love Thee such good things as pass man's understanding; Pour into our hearts such love toward Thee, that we, loving Thee above all things, may obtain Thy prom ises, which exceed all that we can desire; through Jesus Christ our Lord. Amen.

The Seventh Sunday after Trinity.

LORD of all power and might, who art the author and giver of all good things; Graft in our hearts the love of Thy Name, increase in us true religion, nourish us with all goodness, and of Thy great mercy keep us in the same; through Jesus Christ our Lord. Amen.

The Eighth Sunday after Trinity.

O GOD, whose never-failing providence ordereth all things both in heaven and earth; We humbly beseech Thee to put away from us all hurtful things, and to give us those things which are profitable for us; through Jesus Christ our Lord. Amen.

The Ninth Sunday after Trinity.

GRANT to us, Lord, we beseech Thee, the spirit to think and do always such things as are right; that we, who cannot do any thing that is good without Thee, may by Thee be enabled to live according to Thy will; through Jesus Christ our Lord. Amen.

The Tenth Sunday after Trinity.

LET Thy merciful ears, O Lord, be open to the prayers of Thy humble servants; and that they may obtain their petitions make them to ask such things as shall please Thee; through Jesus Christ our Lord. Amen.

The Eleventh Sunday after Trinity.

O GOD, who declarest Thy Almighty power chiefly in showing mercy and pity; Mercifully grant unto us such a measure of Thy grace, that we, running the way of Thy commandments, may obtain Thy gracious promises, and be made partakers of Thy heavenly treasure; through Jesus Christ our Lord. Amen.

The Twelfth Sunday after Trinity.

ALMIGHTY and everlasting God, who art always more ready to hear than we to pray, and art wont to give more than either we desire or deserve; Pour down upon us the abundance of Thy mercy; forgiving us those things whereof our conscience is afraid, and giving us those good things which we are not worthy to ask, but through the merits and mediation of Jesus Christ, Thy Son our Lord. Amen.

The Thirteenth Sunday after Trinity.

ALMIGHTY and merciful God, of whose only gift it cometh that Thy faithful people do unto Thee true and laudable service; Grant, we beseech Thee, that we may so faithfully serve Thee in this life, that we fail not finally to attain Thy heavenly promises; through the merits of Jesus Christ our Lord. Amen.

The Fourteenth Sunday after Trinity.

ALMIGHTY and everlasting God, give unto us the increase of faith, hope, and charity; and, that we may obtain that which Thou dost promise, make us to love that which Thou dost command; through Jesus Christ our Lord. Amen.

COLLECTS AND PRAYERS.

The Fifteenth Sunday after Trinity.

KEEP, we beseech Thee, O Lord, Thy Church with Thy perpetual mercy; and, because the frailty of man without Thee cannot but fall, keep us ever by Thy help from all things hurtful, and lead us to all things profitable to our salvation; through Jesus Christ our Lord. Amen.

The Sixteenth Sunday after Trinity.

O LORD, we beseech Thee, let Thy continual pity cleanse and defend Thy Church; and, because it cannot continue in safety without Thy succour, preserve it evermore by Thy help and goodness; through Jesus Christ our Lord. Amen.

The Seventeenth Sunday after Trinity.

LORD, we pray Thee that Thy grace may always prevent and follow us, and make us continually to be given to all good works; through Jesus Christ our Lord. Amen.

The Eighteenth Sunday after Trinity.

LORD, we beseech Thee, grant Thy people grace to withstand the temptations of the world, the flesh, and the devil; and with pure hearts and minds to follow Thee, the only God; through Jesus Christ our Lord. Amen.

The Nineteenth Sunday after Trinity.

O GOD, forasmuch as without Thee we are not able to please Thee; Mercifully grant that Thy Holy Spirit may in all things direct and rule our hearts; through Jesus Christ our Lord. Amen.

The Twentieth Sunday after Trinity.

O ALMIGHTY and most merciful God, of Thy bountiful goodness keep us, we beseech Thee, from all things that may hurt us; that we, being ready both in body and soul, may cheerfully accomplish those things which Thou commandest; through Jesus Christ our Lord. Amen.

The Twenty-first Sunday after Trinity.

GRANT, we beseech Thee, merciful Lord, to Thy faithful people pardon and peace, that they may be cleansed from all their sins, and serve Thee with a quiet mind; through Jesus Christ our Lord. Amen.

The Twenty-second Sunday after Trinity.

LORD, we beseech Thee to keep Thy household the Church in continual godliness; that through Thy protection it may be free from all adversities, and devoutly given to serve thee in good works, to the glory of Thy Name; through Jesus Christ our Lord. Amen.

The Twenty-third Sunday after Trinity.

O GOD, our refuge and strength, who art the author of all godliness; Be ready, we beseech Thee, to hear the devout prayers of Thy Church; and grant that those things which we ask faithfully we may obtain effectually; through Jesus Christ our Lord. Amen.

COLLECTS AND PRAYERS.

The Twenty-fourth Sunday after Trinity.

O LORD, we beseech Thee, absolve Thy people from their offences; that through Thy bountiful goodness we may all be delivered from the bands of those sins, which by our frailty we have committed. Grant this, O heavenly Father, for Jesus Christ's sake, our blessed Lord and Saviour. *Amen.*

The Twenty-fifth Sunday after Trinity.

STIR up, we beseech Thee, O Lord, the wills of Thy faithful people; that they, plenteously bringing forth the fruit of good works, may by Thee be plenteously rewarded; through Jesus Christ our Lord. *Amen.*

Saint Andrew's Day.

ALMIGHTY God, who didst give such grace unto Thy holy Apostle Saint Andrew, that he readily obeyed the calling of Thy Son Jesus Christ, and followed Him without delay; Grant unto us all, that we, being called by Thy holy Word, may forthwith give up ourselves obediently to fulfil Thy holy commandments; through the same Jesus Christ our Lord. *Amen.*

Saint Thomas the Apostle.

ALMIGHTY and everliving God, who, for the greater confirmation of the faith, didst suffer Thy holy Apostle Thomas to be doubtful in Thy Son's resurrection; Grant us so perfectly, and without all doubt, to believe in Thy Son Jesus Christ, that our faith in Thy sight may never be reproved. Hear us, O Lord, through the same Jesus Christ, to whom, with Thee and the Holy Ghost, be all honour and glory, now and for evermore. *Amen.*

Saint Stephen's Day.

GRANT, O Lord, that, in all our sufferings here upon earth for the testimony of Thy truth, we may steadfastly look up to heaven, and by faith behold the glory that shall be revealed; and, being filled with the Holy Ghost, may learn to love and bless our persecutors by the example of Thy first Martyr Saint Stephen, who prayed for his murderers to Thee, O blessed Jesus, who standest at the right hand of God to succour all those who suffer for Thee, our only Mediator and Advocate. *Amen.*

Saint John the Evangelist's Day.

MERCIFUL Lord, we beseech Thee to cast Thy bright beams of light upon Thy Church, that it being instructed by the doctrine of Thy blessed Apostle and Evangelist Saint John, may so walk in the light of Thy truth, that it may at length attain to everlasting life; through Jesus Christ our Lord. *Amen.*

The Innocents' Day.

O ALMIGHTY God, who out of the mouths of babes and sucklings hast ordained strength, and madest infants to glorify Thee by their deaths; Mortify and kill all vices in us, and so strengthen us by Thy grace, that by the innocency of our lives, and constancy of our faith even unto death, we may glorify Thy holy Name; through Jesus Christ our Lord. *Amen.*

COLLECTS AND PRAYERS.

The Conversion of Saint Paul.

O GOD, who, through the preaching of the blessed Apostle Saint Paul, hast caused the light of the Gospel to shine throughout the world; Grant, we beseech Thee, that we, having his wonderful conversion in remembrance, may show forth our thankfulness unto Thee for the same, by following the holy doctrine which he taught; through Jesus Christ our Lord. *Amen.*

The Presentation of Christ in the Temple, commonly called, The Purification of Saint Mary the Virgin.

ALMIGHTY and everliving God, we humbly beseech Thy Majesty, that as Thy onlybegotten Son was this day presented in the Temple in substance of our flesh, so we may be presented unto Thee with pure and clean hearts, by the same Thy Son Jesus Christ our Lord. *Amen.*

Saint Matthias's Day.

O ALMIGHTY God, who into the place of the traitor Judas didst choose Thy faithful servant Matthias to be of the number of the twelve Apostles; Grant that Thy Church, being alway preserved from false Apostles, may be ordered and guided by faithful and true pastors; through Jesus Christ our Lord. *Amen.*

The Annunciation of the Blessed Virgin Mary.

WE beseech Thee, O Lord, pour Thy grace into our hearts; that as we have known the incarnation of Thy Son Jesus Christ by the message of an Angel, so by His cross and passion we may be brought unto the glory of His resurrection; through the same Jesus Christ our Lord. *Amen.*

Saint Mark's Day.

O ALMIGHTY God, who hast instructed Thy holy Church with the heavenly doctrine of Thy Evangelist Saint Mark; Give us grace that, being not like children carried away with every blast of vain doctrine, we may be established in the truth of Thy holy Gospel; through Jesus Christ our Lord. *Amen.*

Saint Philip and Saint James's Day.

O ALMIGHTY God, whom truly to know is everlasting life; Grant us perfectly to know Thy Son Jesus Christ to be the way, the truth, and the life; that, following the steps of Thy holy Apostles Saint Philip and Saint James, we may steadfastly walk in the way that leadeth to eternal life; through the same Thy Son Jesus Christ our Lord. *Amen.*

Saint Barnabas the Apostle.

O LORD God Almighty, who didst endue Thy holy Apostle Barnabas with singular gifts of the Holy Ghost; Leave us not, we beseech Thee, destitute of Thy manifold gifts, nor yet of grace to use them alway to Thy honour and glory; through Jesus Christ our Lord. *Amen.*

Saint John Baptist's Day.

ALMIGHTY God, by whose providence Thy servant John Baptist was wonderfully born, and sent to prepare the way of Thy Son our Saviour, by preaching repentance; make us so to follow his doctrine and holy life, that we may truly repent according to his preaching; and after his example constantly speak the truth, boldly rebuke vice, and patiently suffer for the truth's sake; through Jesus Christ our Lord. Amen.

Saint Peter's Day.

O ALMIGHTY God, who by Thy Son Jesus Christ didst give to Thy Apostle Saint Peter many excellent gifts, and commandedst him earnestly to feed Thy flock; Make, we beseech Thee, all Bishops and Pastors diligently to preach Thy holy Word, and the people obediently to follow the same, that they may receive the crown of everlasting glory; through Jesus Christ our Lord. Amen.

Saint James the Apostle.

GRANT, O merciful God, that as Thine holy Apostle Saint James, leaving his father and all that he had, without delay was obedient unto the calling of Thy Son Jesus Christ, and followed Him; so we, forsaking all worldly and carnal affections, may be evermore ready to follow Thy holy commandments; through Jesus Christ our Lord. Amen.

Saint Bartholomew the Apostle.

O ALMIGHTY and everlasting God, who didst give to Thine Apostle Bartholomew grace truly to believe and to preach Thy Word; Grant, we beseech Thee, unto Thy Church, to love that Word which he believed, and both to preach and receive the same; through Jesus Christ our Lord. Amen.

Saint Matthew the Apostle.

O ALMIGHTY God, who by Thy blessed Son didst call Matthew from the receipt of custom to be an Apostle and Evangelist; Grant us grace to forsake all covetous desires, and inordinate love of riches, and to follow the same Thy Son Jesus Christ, who liveth and reigneth with Thee and the Holy Ghost, one God, world without end. Amen.

Saint Michael and All Angels.

O EVERLASTING God, who hast ordained and constituted the services of Angels and men in a wonderful order; Mercifully grant, that as Thy holy Angels always do Thee service in heaven, so, by Thy appointment, they may succour and defend us on earth; through Jesus Christ our Lord. Amen.

Saint Luke the Evangelist.

ALMIGHTY God, who calledst Luke the Physician, whose praise is in the Gospel, to be an Evangelist, and Physician of the soul; May it please Thee, that, by the wholesome medicines of the doctrine delivered by him, all the diseases of our souls may be healed; through the merits of Thy Son Jesus Christ our Lord. Amen.

Saint Simon and Saint Jude, Apostles.

O ALMIGHTY God, who hast built Thy Church upon the foundation of the Apostles and Prophets, Jesus Christ Himself being the head corner-stone; Grant us so to be joined together in unity of spirit by their doctrine, that we may be made an holy temple acceptable unto Thee; through Jesus Christ our Lord. *Amen.*

All Saint's Day.

O ALMIGHTY God, who hast knit together Thine elect in one communion and fellowship, in the mystical body of Thy Son Christ our Lord; Grant us grace so to follow Thy blessed Saints in all virtuous and godly living, that we may come to those unspeakable joys, which Thou hast prepared for those who unfeignedly love Thee; through Jesus Christ our Lord. *Amen.*

ANCIENT ORISONS FOR THE HOURS.

At Matins.

O LORD, who grieved for their afflictions, didst lead Thy people out of the darkness of Egypt, and vouchsafe to deliver them by the hand of Thy servant: do Thou grant also unto us Thy servants, that delivered from the darkness of this world, we may be allowed to enter into that rest which Thou hast promised to our fathers, through our Lord Jesus Christ. *Amen.*

At the Third Hour.

O LORD Jesus Christ, who, at the third hour of the day, wast led forth to the pain of the cross for the salvation of the world: I suppliantly beseech Thee to blot out mine offences: and may I deserve to obtain forgiveness with Thee for my past sins, and watch strictly against all future transgressions, who with the Father and the Holy Ghost livest and reignest God, world without end. *Amen.*

O LORD, Father Almighty, we humbly entreat the glory of Thy Majesty, that as at the third hour Thou didst strengthen Thine apostles by the divine visitation of Thy Spirit: so by His coming, Thou wouldst vouchsafe to illumine and keep our hearts, through our Lord Jesus Christ. *Amen.*

At the Sixth Hour.

O LORD Jesus Christ, who, when for the redemption of the world, Thou didst at the sixth hour ascend the tree of the Cross, the whole world was turned back into darkness: shed forth such light upon my soul and body, that I may be worthy to attain eternal life: who livest and reignest God, for ever and ever. *Amen.*

WE humbly beseech Thy holy and terrible Name, O Lord Almighty, who, at the sixth hour of the day, didst will Thy most glorious Son, our Lord, to ascend the Cross to deliver us from the power of the most wicked enemy; Grant, we pray Thee, that redeemed by this His cross, we may at all times serve Thee righteously without offence, through the same our Lord Jesus Christ. *Amen.*

At the Ninth Hour.

O LORD Jesus Christ, who, at the ninth hour in Thine agony on the Cross, didst command the believing thief to pass within the walls of paradise, I humbly beseech Thee to grant that, confessing my sins, I may after my death enter with gladness into the joys of paradise: who with the Father and the Holy Spirit, livest and reignest God, world without end. *Amen.*

At the Hour of Vespers.

I THANK Thee, O Lord Almighty God, who hast permitted me through the course of this day to reach this Vesper hour, and I humbly beseech Thee, that the lifting up of my hands to Thee, may be in Thy sight an acceptable evening sacrifice, through our Lord Jesus Christ. *Amen.*

O LORD, who hast wrought out our salvation in the midst of the earth, with whom the darkness is not dark, but the night is as clear as the day; lighten our darkness, we beseech Thee, O Lord, so that passing a peaceful and quiet night, in the morning hours we may rise again to Thy praises, through our Lord Jesus Christ. *Amen.*

ENLIGHTEN our night, we entreat Thee, Almighty Lord, and cause Thy servants ever to sleep from their sins: so that awake to the virtues of the angels, and safe from every evil, we may by Thy help be worthy to attain the clear day through our Lord Jesus Christ. *Amen.*

At the Hour of Compline.

O LORD God, the Ruler and Protector of all men, who hast divided the light from the darkness, I beseech Thee with the prayer of faith, that through the darkness of the coming night, Thy right hand may protect me, and that I may rise again with joy in the light of the morning, through our Lord Jesus Christ. *Amen.*

Orison of St. Augustine, in the Night.

O GOD our Father, who dost exhort us to pray, and who dost grant what we ask, if only when we ask we live a better life: hear me who am trembling in this darkness, and stretch out Thy right hand unto me: hold forth Thy light before me: recall me from my error, and Thou being my guide, may I be restored to myself and to Thee, through Jesus Christ. *Amen.*

PRAYERS.

I. *For the Church.*

ALMIGHTY and everlasting God, who hast in Christ revealed Thy glory unto all nations; protect the works of Thy mercy, that the Church spread throughout the world may abide with steadfast faith in the confession of Thy Name. Through the same.

O GOD, who hast vouchsafed to raise up in every age defenders of Thy Church, to put down her enemies, and to restore the solemnities of Thy holy service; grant that we following their footsteps may so abide in Thy service, that overcoming all the snares of our enemies, we may rejoice in perpetual peace. Through.

PRAYERS.

O GOD, the might of them that hope in Thee, who hast strengthened Thy saints with the gift of constancy to defend the liberties of Thy Church; grant that we may valiantly strive against and overcome all obstacles. Through.

II. *For the Bishop of the Diocese.*

GRANT, O Lord, to Thy servant N..., whom Thou hast set over Thy flock in this diocese, the spirit of counsel and might, the spirit of wisdom and piety, that through the holy conversation of their bishop the devotion of the faithful may increase, and that the salvation of the flock may be the joy and crown of the shepherd. Through.

III. *For Harmony with Fellow-workers.*

O GOD, who art Love, grant to Thy children who eat of Thy bread to bear one another's burdens in perfect goodwill, that Thy peace which passeth all understanding may keep our hearts and minds in Christ Jesus our Lord. Who.

O GOD, who makest men to be of one mind in an house, take away from us all cause of dissension, that we may keep the unity of the Spirit in the bond of peace. Through.

O LORD, grant that Thy servants who are gathered together in Thy Name, and who eat of the same bread, may with one mind endeavour to provoke one another to love and to good works, that by their holy conversation the sweet savour of Christ may be shed abroad. Through the same.

IV. *For those engaged in Works of Mercy.*

BLESS, O Lord, we beseech Thee, all those who are devoted to serve Thee in works of charity as well for the training of the young as for the reclaiming of the fallen [especially...]. Also those who are occupied in visiting the sick, the poor, and the ignorant [especially...]. Accept their labours and grant that while they sympathize with others in their necessity and sorrow, they may bring them to share the joy of the divine life wherein they live, and may with them attain to that fulness of spiritual perfection which they desire. Through.

V. *For Benefactors.*

HEAR us, O merciful and gracious God, beseeching Thee for all Thy Faithful who have bestowed their alms upon us: regard not our sins but their faith, who in the faith of Thy Name have given to us of their temporal goods.

THOU, O God, who requitest all good works, repay them much for little, and eternal promises for earthly gifts, O Saviour of the world. Who livest.

VI. *For Friends.*

O GOD, who hast poured the gift of charity into the hearts of Thy faithful people through the grace of the Holy Spirit, grant unto Thy servants [....], for whom we entreat Thy mercy, health of soul and body, that they may love Thee with all their strength, and with all their love accomplish Thy will. Through.

VII. *For School Children.*

POUR down Thy blessing, O heavenly Father, upon those children whom Thou hast committed to our charge, and give us grace to train them in Thy faith, fear, and love, that as they grow in years they may grow in grace, and may hereafter be found in the number of Thy elect children. Through.

VIII. *For Penitents.*

POUR, we beseech Thee, O Lord, the spirit of grace and prayer upon Thy servants [especially . . .], that looking upon Jesus lifted up upon the Cross, where they have nailed Him by their sins, they may feel true sorrow, may be healed quickly, and live. Through the same.

IX. *For Returning Penitents.*

O GOD, who, by the blood of Thine only Son didst redeem mankind from the power of death; quicken, we beseech Thee, the souls of all returning penitents [especially . . . .], and receive upon their return those whom Thou didst recall when they were wandering. Hear their sighs, heal their wounds, strengthen their weakness. Grant them with such contrition to confess their sins, that in the day of judgment they may be found worthy of Thy glory never more to be lost, as they have been restored by Thy love to the grace which they had forfeited. Hear us, we beseech Thee, for Jesus Christ's sake, our Lord.

X. *For those exposed to Temptations.*

O GOD, who willest not the death of a sinner, protect with Thy heavenly aid those who are exposed to special temptations [. . . .]; and grant that, in the fulfilment of Thy commandments, they may be strengthened by the assistance of Thy grace. Through.

O WHO justifiest the wicked and desirest not the death of a sinner; we humbly beseech Thy Majesty mercifully to defend with Thy divine protection Thy servants who put their trust in Thee, and keep them ever under Thy safeguard, that they may always serve Thee, and not be separated from Thee by any temptations. Through.

XI. *For the Lapsed.*

O GOD of mercy, pity, and pardon, God of love and peace, who of Thy tenderness for mankind didst stretch forth Thy hands upon the Cross, who didst call the Canaanitish woman and the publican to repentance; vouchsafe to convert Thy sinful servants, grant that they may confess their guilt before Thy holy altar, and humbly seek remission of their sins. Mercifully grant them time for repentance, fruits meet thereof, and a profitable end in true contrition. Who.

GRANT, we beseech Thee, O Lord, to those who have wandered out of the way through sin, that they may obtain pardon for their offences, and be restored cleansed to Thy holy Church. Through.

O GOD, merciful and gracious, hear our prayers, which we offer in sorrow before Thee for our perishing *brother*, that, turned from the error of *his* ways, *he* may be delivered from death, and that where sin abounds, grace may much more abound. Through.

O LORD Jesus Christ, the Good Shepherd, who feedest with Thine own body those sheep which Thou hast purchased with Thine own blood; mercifully seek out Thy lost sheep, and bringing it back to the fold make it fit for the eternal pastures. Who livest.

XII. *For the Faithful Departed.*

O LORD our Redeemer, who hast purchased mankind by Thine own blood, ransoming us by Thy death from the sting of death, and giving us everlasting life by Thy resurrection; grant rest unto all who have fallen asleep in holiness, in the desert or in the cities, at sea or on land, and in all places, to kings and priests and bishops, to the solitary and the wedded, to all ages and generations, and fit them for Thy heavenly kingdom. Where Thou livest and reignest.

O LORD, Fountain of Life, who by Thy divine manhood dost set free captives; mercifully grant unto Thy servants who pass hence to Thee in faith a dwelling-place in the joy of paradise. Where.

O LORD our Saviour, who dost feed Thy faithful people in a green pasture, and leadest them to the waters of comfort, turn not away Thy servants from that pleasant land of rest. Where.

OFFICE OF INTERCESSION.

FOR SISTERHOODS AND SIMILAR ASSOCIATIONS.

LET us make our humble prayers to Almighty God, beseeching His mercy for all the world: let us pray for the good estate of the Catholic Church and for the peace of all nations of men; for this house and all that are therein, and especially for the [*sisterhood, confraternity, order,—naming it*], and for the welfare of all its friends and benefactors; for our brethren and sisters, and all those under our care, with all that have done us good, and for all true Christian people: and that it may please Him to multiply unto us fellow-helpers, to the glory of His Holy Name and to the comfort and relief of such as be in trouble, sorrow, need, sickness, or any other adversity, in the midst of this evil world.

Deus Misereatur. Ps. lxvi.

GOD, be merciful unto us and bless us: and shew us the light of His countenance, and be merciful unto us.

That Thy way may be known upon earth: Thy saving health among all nations.

Let the people praise Thee, O God; yea, let all the people praise Thee.

O let the nations rejoice and be glad: for Thou shalt judge the folk righteously, and govern the nations upon earth.

Let the people praise Thee, O God: yea, let all the people praise Thee.

Then shall the earth bring forth her increase: and God, even our own God, shall give us His blessing.

God shall bless us: and all the ends of the world shall fear Him.

Glory be to the Father, &c.

LORD, have mercy.
Christ, have mercy.
Lord, have mercy.
Our Father, &c.

℣. O Lord, show Thy mercy upon us.

℟. And grant us Thy salvation.

℣. Send blessing upon Thy people.

℟. Govern them and lift them up for ever.

℣. Let there be peace in Thy strength, O Lord.

℟. And plenteousness within Thy towers.

℣. O Lord, hear our prayer.

℟. And let our cry come unto Thee.

The Lord be with you.
And with Thy spirit.

Let us pray.

GOD, who, through the grace of Thy Holy Spirit, dost pour the gifts of charity into the hearts of Thy faithful people: grant to Thy servants and handmaidens, for whom we beseech Thy clemency, health both of mind and body: that they may love Thee with their whole strength, and with joyfulness may perform those things which are pleasing unto Thee, and grant us Thy peace in our time, through Christ our Lord. *Amen.*

O LORD, who didst send the seventy disciples before Thy face into every city and place whither Thou Thyself wouldst come: mercifully regard our labours, multiply unto us fellow-helpers in the same, and so prosper the work of our hands upon us, that when Thou comest again, Thou mayest find all things ready for Thee, who livest and reignest, world without end. *Amen.*

ALMIGHTY and merciful God, builder and keeper of the heavenly Jerusalem, build up and keep our dwellings and their inhabitants, that the home of peace and quiet may be in them. Through Jesus Christ our Lord. *Amen.*

℣. Stablish the thing, O Lord, that Thou hast wrought in us.

℟. For Thy temple's sake at Jerusalem.

℣. Let us depart in peace.

℟. In the Name of the Lord. *Amen.*

V.

HYMNS.

HYMNS.

ADVENT.

I.

BEHOLD the Bridegroom cometh in the middle of the night,
  And blest is he whose loins are girt, whose lamp is burning bright;
But woe to that dull servant, whom his Master shall surprise,
With lamp untrimmed, unburning, and with slumber in his eyes.

Do thou, my soul, beware, beware lest thou in sleep sink down,
Lest thou be given o'er to death, and lose the golden crown:
But see that thou be sober, with watchful eye, and thus
Cry — Holy, Holy, Holy GOD, have mercy upon us.

That day, the day of fear, shall come; my soul, slack not thy toil,
But light thy lamp and feed it well, and make it bright with oil;
Who knowest not how soon may sound the cry at eventide, —
Behold, the Bridegroom comes. Arise! Go forth to meet the Bride.

Beware, my soul; take thou good heed, lest thou in slumber lie,
And, like the five, remain without, and knock, and vainly cry;
But watch, and bear thy lamp undimmed, and Christ shall gird thee on
His own bright wedding-robe of light — the Glory of the Son.

CHRISTMAS.

II.

ROYAL Day that chasest gloom!
  Day by gladness speeded!
Thou beheld'st from Mary's womb
  How the King proceeded;

HYMNS.

Whom, True Man, with praise our choir
Hails, and love, and heart's desire,
  Joy and admiration;
Who, True GOD, enthroned in light,
Passeth wonder, passeth sight,
  Passeth cogitation.

On the Virgin as He hung,
  GOD, the world's Creator,
Like a rose from lily sprung,—
  Stood astounded nature:
That a Maiden's arms enfold
Him that made the world of old,
  Him that ever liveth:
That a Maiden's spotless breast
To the King Eternal rest,
  Warmth, and nurture giveth!

As the sunbeam through the glass
  Passeth but not staineth,
Thus the Virgin, as she was,
  Virgin still remaineth:
Blessed Mother, in whose womb
Lay the Light that exiles gloom,
  GOD, the Lord of Ages;
Blessed Maid! from whom the Lord
Her own Infant, GOD adored
  Hunger's pangs assuages.

PASSION-TIDE.

III.

CHRIST, on whose Face the soldiers
  Spat in their mockery;
Who hangedst, faint and bleeding,
  On the atoning Tree;
Who heardest the revilings
  Of them that cursed Thy Name,
And watched, in bitter hatred,
  Beneath the Cross of Shame;

Look down, we pray, in mercy
  On weary souls below.

Who turn to Thee, their Saviour,
  For comfort in their woe;
O let their piteous crying
  Pierce through the angels' song,
That cry of desolation,
  "How long, O Lord, how long?"

Christ, who art throned in heaven,
  Supremest over all,
Before whose Face archangels
  In adoration fall;
Who hearest the sweet singing
  Of them that tell Thy fame,
And tread, amid their harpings,
  The sea of glass and flame;

O lift us, by Thy Passion,
  Up from the bed of sin;
O bring us, by Thy Rising,
  The heavenly gates within;
That, with the angel choirs,
  We there may raise the strain
Of glory, laud, and honour,
  To Thee, for sinners slain.

IV.

WHEN our heads are bowed with woe,
  When our bitter tears o'erflow,
When we mourn the lost, the dear,
JESU, Son of Mary, hear.

Thou our throbbing flesh hast worn,
Thou our mortal griefs hast borne,
Thou hast shed the human tear;
JESU, Son of Mary, hear.

When the solemn death-bell tolls,
For our own departing souls,
When our final doom is near,
JESU, Son of Mary, hear.

Thou hast bowed the dying head,
Thou the blood of life hast shed,

HYMNS.

Thou hast filled a mortal bier;
Jesu, Son of Mary, hear.

When the heart is sad within
With the thought of all its sin;
When the spirit shrinks with fear,
Jesu, Son of Mary, hear.

Thou the shame, the grief, hast known
Though the Sins were not Thine own;
Thou hast deigned their load to bear,
Jesu, Son of Mary, hear.   Amen.

V.

LORD Jesu, by Thy Passion,
  To Thee I make my prayer,
Thou who in mercy smitest,
  Have mercy, Lord, and spare.

O wash me in the fountain
  That floweth from Thy Side,
O clothe me in the raiment
  Thy Blood hath purified.

O hold Thou up my goings,
  And lead from strength to strength,
That unto Thee in Sion
  I may appear at length.

O hearken to my knocking,
  And open wide the door,
That I may enter freely,
  And never leave Thee more.

O bring me, loving Jesu,
  To that most blessed place,
Where angels and archangels
  Look ever on Thy Face.

Where gladsome Alleluias
  Unceasingly resound,
Where martyrs, now triumphant,
  Walk robed in white, and crowned.

HYMNS.

O make my spirit worthy
  To join that ransomed throng,
O teach my lips to utter
  That everlasting song.

O give that last, best blessing
  That even Saints can know,
To follow in Thy footsteps
  Wherever Thou dost go.

Not wisdom, might, or glory,
  I ask to win above;
I ask for Thee, Thee only,
  O Thou Eternal Love.

VI.

O JESU, in thy torture
  Nailed to the bitter tree,
My soul's true guide and nurture,
  I yearn to be with Thee.

How can I taste of pleasure,
  Whilst Thou dost hang in pain,
JESU, mine only treasure,
  Mine everlasting gain?

O JESU, may Thy sadness,
  Thine agony and tears,
Win for my spirit gladness
  Throughout the endless years.

With Thine own Body feed me,
  Life to my soul accord,
Then to Thy pierced heart lead me,
  And hide me there, O Lord.

And in my dying hour,
  By those sharp wounds I pray,
Lord, may Thy Passion's power
  Wash all my sins away

HYMNS.

VII.

LORD, who in pain and weariness
　Thy path of sorrow here didst tread;
Who, scorned of men and shelterless,
　Couldst find no place to lay Thy Head;
　　Grant Thy shelter, JESU meek,
　　To Thy poor, who refuge seek.

Lord, who through long and saddened years,
　Didst toil for suffering mankind;
Didst bind their wounds, didst calm their fears,
　Didst cure the sick, the halt, the blind,
　　Grant Thy healing, JESU blest,
　　To the faint who long for rest.

Lord, who wast merciful to spare,
　And madest leprous sinners clean,
Who freely, at her tearful prayer,
　Forgavest Mary Magdalene,
　　Grant Thy pardon, JESU sweet,
　　To the mourners at Thy Feet.

Lord, who didst die upon the Rood,
　That we might ever die to sin,
Who givest us Thyself as Food,
　To make us strong the goal to win;
　　Grant Thy patience, JESU dear,
　　Unto all who suffer here.

Lord, who from burial didst arise,
　That we might rise to life in Thee,
And hence ascending to the skies,
　Dost rule all things in majesty;
　　Grant Thy glory, JESU pure,
　　To the faithful who endure.

VIII.

St. John xx. 15.

AS the Gardener Him addressing,
　Well and rightly she believed:
He, the Sower, gave His blessing
　To the seed her heart received:

HYMNS.

Not at first His Form confessing,
  Soon His Voice her soul perceiv'd.

She beheld, as yet not knowing
  In the mystical disguise,
CHRIST, that in her breast was sowing
  Deep and heavenly mysteries:
Till His Voice, her name bestowing,
  Bade her hear and recognize.

She to JESUS, JESUS weepeth,
  Of her Lord removed complains;
JESUS in her breast she keepeth;
  JESUS seeks, yet still retains;
He that soweth, He that reapeth
  All her heart, unknown remains.

Why, kind JESU, why thus hiding,
  When thyself Thou wouldst reveal?
Why, in Mary's breast abiding,
  From her love thyself conceal?
Why, True Light, in her residing,
  Can she not its radiance feel?

O how strangely Thou eludest
  Souls that on Thee have believ'd!
But eluding, ne'er deludest,
  Nor deceiv'st, nor art deceiv'd;
But including, still excludest;
  Fully known, yet not perceiv'd.

Laud to Thee, and praise for ever,
  Life, Hope, Light of every soul!
Through Thy merits may we never
  Be inscrib'd in Death's dark roll,
But with Mary's true endeavor
  All our sins, like her, condole. Amen.

THE FEASTS OF THE BLESSED VIRGIN MARY.

IX.

VIRGIN-BORN! we bow before Thee!
  Blessed was the womb that bore Thee!

HYMNS.

Mary, Mother meek and mild,
Blessed was she in her Child!

Blessed was the breast that fed Thee!
Blessed was the hand that led Thee!
Blessed was the parent's eye,
That watch'd Thy slumb'ring infancy!

Virgin-born! we bow before Thee!
Blessed was the womb that bore Thee!
Mary, Virgin-mother mild,
Blessed was she in her Child!

Honor, laud, and glory be
JESU, Virgin-born, to Thee;
To the FATHER, as is meet
And the Blessed PARACLETE. Amen.

THE FEAST OF AN APOSTLE.

X.

TH' Eternal gifts of CHRIST the King,
Th' Apostles' glorious deeds we sing;
And while due hymns of praise we pay,
Our thankful hearts cast grief away.

The Church in these her princes boasts,
These victor-chiefs of warrior hosts;
The soldiers of the heavenly hall,
The lights that rose on earth for all.

'T was thus the yearning faith of Saints
Th' unconquer'd hope that never faints,
The love of CHRIST that knows not shame
The Prince of this world overcame.

In these the FATHER's glory shone,
In these the will of GOD the SON;
In these exults the HOLY GHOST,
Through these rejoice the Heavenly Host.

Redeemer,-hear us of Thy love,
That with this glorious band above,
Hereafter, of Thine endless grace,
Thy Servants also may have place. Amen.

HYMNS.

THE FEAST OF A MARTYR.
XI.

BLESSED Feasts of Blessed Martyrs!
   Saintly days of saintly men!
With affection's recollections,
   Greet we your return again.

Mighty deeds they wrought, and wonders,
   While a frame of flesh they bore:
We with meetest praise, and sweetest,
   Honor them for ever more.

Faith unblenching, Hope unquenching,
   Well-lov'd Lord, and single heart, —
Thus they glorious and victorious
   Bore the Martyr's happy part.

Blood in slaughter pour'd like water,
   Torments long and heavy chain,
Flame, and axe, and laceration,
   They endur'd, and conquer'd pain.

While they passed through divers tortures,
   Till they sank by death oppress'd,
Earth's rejected were elected,
   To have portion with the Blest.

By contempt of worldly pleasures,
   And by mighty battles done,
They have reached the Land of Angels,
   And with them are knit in one.

They are made co-heirs of glory,
   And they sit with CHRIST on high:
O that, as He heard their weeping,
   He may also hear our cry;

Till, this weary life completed,
   And its many labors past,
He shall grant us to be seated
   In our Father's Home at last! Amen.

HYMNS.

ALL SAINTS' DAY.

XII.

IF there be that skills to reckon
  All the number of the blest,
He, perchance, can weigh the gladness
  Of the everlasting rest
Which, their earthly warfare finish'd,
  They through suffering have possess'd.

Through the vale of lamentation
  Happily and safely past,
Now the years of their affliction
  In their memory they recast,
And the end of all perfection
  They can contemplate at last.

While their cruel Tempter duly
  Suffers torments evermore,
To the Saviour that redeem'd them
  Those redeemed ones praises pour;
And the Monarch that rewards them
  Those rewarded Saints adore.

In a glass, through types and riddles,
  Dwelling here, we see alone;
There serenely, purely, clearly,
  We shall know as we are known;
Fixing our enlighten'd vision
  On the glory of the Throne.

There the Trinity of Persons
  Unbeclouded shall we see;
There the unity of essence
  Shall reveal'd in glory be;
While we hail the Threefold Godhead,
  And the Simple Unity.

Wherefore, man, take heart and courage,
  Whatsoe'er thy present pain;
Such untold reward through suffering
  Thou hereafter mayst attain;
And forever in His glory
  With the Light of Light to reign.

HYMNS.

Laud and honour to the FATHER;
  Laud and honour to the SON;
Laud and honour to the SPIRIT;
  Ever Three and ever One:
Consubstantial, Co-eternal,
  While unending ages run. Amen.

THE HOLY EUCHARIST.
XIII.

OF the glorious Body telling,
  O, my tongue, its mysteries sing;
And the Blood, all price excelling,
  Which for this world's ransoming
In a generous womb once dwelling,
  He shed forth, the Gentiles' King.

Given for us, for us descending
  Of a Virgin to proceed,
Man with man in converse blending
  Scattered He the Gospel seed;
Till His sojourn drew to ending,
  Which He closed in wondrous deed.

At the last Great Supper seated,
  Circled by His brethren's band,
All the Law required, completed,
  In the feast its statutes planned,
To the Twelve Himself He meted
  For their food with His own hand.

WORD made Flesh, by Word he maketh
  Very Bread His Flesh to be;
Man in wine CHRIST's Blood partaketh,
  And if senses fail to see,
Faith alone the true heart waketh
  To behold the Mystery.

Therefore we before it bending,
  This great Sacrament adore;
Types and shadows have their ending
  In the new Rite evermore:
Faith, our outward sense amending,
  Maketh good defects before.

HYMNS.

Honour, laud, and praise addressing
　To the FATHER and the SON,
Might ascribe we, virtue, blessing,
　And eternal benison;
HOLY GHOST, from both progressing
　Equal laud to Thee be done.　Amen.

XIV.

CHRIST, the Light that knows no waning,
　Gives to us His Flesh as food,
Drink He gives us also, deigning
　To refresh us with His Blood.

CHRIST, Thou radiance ever glowing,
　Who upon the Cross didst bleed,
Light on all Thy saints bestowing,
　With Thyself Thy flock dost feed.

Flesh which we are now receiving,
　Of a Virgin took the WORD,
And the Blood we drink believing,
　He for sinful man outpoured.

In this rite, our souls to nourish,
　To the WORD made Flesh we come;
Hence our faith in strength doth flourish,
　Hence we reach our heavenly home.

Bread of sweetness, ever holy,
　Full art Thou of pure delight;
Saviour, born of Maiden lowly,
　King art Thou of perfect might.

May we ever eat in gladness,
　Of this rich angelic Bread,
May we in death's hour of sadness,
　With this sweetest gift be fed.

He was at the third day-hour
　Led a Victim forth to die,
When He bare His Cross of power.

HYMNS.

Lead us, Giver of Salvation,
  To our home Thyself beside,
Where eternal jubilation
  Dwelleth through the Lamb that died.

Evermore we there the story
  Of thy wondrous deeds will raise;
Reigning with Thy saints in glory,
  We will offer gifts of praise.

Sacrifice and hymns in union,
  GOD we bring this festal day,
May He with divine Communion
  Feed us in His love for aye. Amen.

XV.

THEE we adore, O hidden Saviour, Thee,
  Who in Thy sacrament dost deign to be;
Both flesh and spirit at Thy presence fail,
Yet here Thy presence we devoutly hail.

O blest Memorial of our dying Lord,
Who living Bread to men doth here afford!
O may our souls for ever feed on Thee,
And Thou, O CHRIST, for ever precious be.

Fountain of goodness, JESU, Lord and GOD,
Cleanse us, unclean, with Thy most cleansing Blood;
Increase our faith and love, that we may know
The hope and peace which from Thy presence flow.

O CHRIST, whom now beneath a veil we see,
May what we thirst for soon our portion be:
To gaze on Thee, and see with unveiled face
The vision of Thy glory and Thy grace. Amen.

VESPER HYMN.
XVI.

SWEET Saviour, bless us ere we go;
  Thy Word into our minds instil;
And make our lukewarm hearts to glow

HYMNS.

With lowly love and fervent will.
Through life's long day and death's dark night,
O gentle JESU, be our light.

The day is gone, its hours are run,
   And Thou hast taken count of all,
The scanty triumphs grace hath won,
   The broken vow, the frequent fall.
Through life's long day and death's dark night,
O gentle JESU, be our light.

Grant us, dear Lord, from evil ways
   True absolution and release;
And bless us, more than in past days,
   With purity and inward peace.
Through life's long day and death's dark night,
O gentle JESU, be our light.

Do more than pardon; give us joy,
   Sweet fear and sober liberty,
And simple hearts without alloy,
   That only long to be like Thee.
Through life's long day and death's dark night,
O gentle JESU, be our light.

Labour is sweet, for Thou hast toiled;
   And care is light, for Thou hast cared;
Ah! never let our works be soiled
   With strife, or by deceit ensnared.
Through life's long day and death's dark night,
O gentle JESU, be our light.

For all we love, the poor, the sad,
   The sinful, unto Thee we call;
O let Thy mercy make us glad;
   Thou art our JESUS, and our All.
Through life's long day and death's dark night,
O gentle JESU, be our light. Amen.

SATURDAY EVENING HYMN.

XVII.

O WHAT their joy
and their glory must be, —

HYMNS.

Those endless Sabbaths
   the blessed ones see!
Crown for the valiant:
   to weary ones rest:
God shall be all,
   and in all ever blest.

What are the Monarch,
   His court and His throne?
What are the peace
   and the joy that they own?
Tell us, ye blest ones,
   that in it have share,
If what ye feel
   ye can fully declare.

Truly "Jerusalem"
   name we that shore,
"Vision of Peace"
   that brings joy evermore!
Wish and fulfilment
   can sever'd be ne'er;
Nor the thing pray'd for
   come short of the prayer.

We, where no trouble
   distraction can bring,
Safely the anthems
   of Sion shall sing:
While for Thy grace, Lord,
   their voices of praise
Thy blessed people
   shall evermore raise.

There dawns no Sabbath,
   no Sabbath is o'er;
Those Sabbath-keepers
   have one, and no more;
One and unending
   is that triumph-song
Which to the Angels
   and us shall belong.

Now in the meanwhile,
   with hearts raised on high,

HYMNS.

We for that Country
    must yearn and must sigh;
Seeking Jerusalem,
    dear native land,
Through our long exile
    on Babylon's strand.

Low before Him
    with our praises we fall,
Of Whom and *in* Whom,
    and *through* Whom are all:
Of Whom, — the FATHER;
    and in Whom, — the SON;
Through Whom, — the SPIRIT,
    with These ever One.   Amen.

THE RELIGIOUS LIFE.

XVIII.

ART thou weary, art thou languid,
    Art thou sore distress'd?
"Come to Me," saith One, "and coming,
            Be at rest!"

Hath He marks to lead me to Him,
    If He be my Guide?
"In His Feet and Hands are wound-prints,
            And His Side."

Is there Diadem, as Monarch,
    That His Brow adorns?
"Yea, a Crown, in very surety,
            But of Thorns!"

If I find Him, if I follow,
    What His guerdon here?
"Many a sorrow, many a labour,
            Many a tear."

If I still hold closely to Him,
    What hath He at last?
"Sorrow vanquish'd, labour ended,
            Jordan passed!"

HYMNS.

If I ask Him to receive me,
  Will He say me nay?
"Not till earth and not till heaven
      Pass away!"

Finding, following, keeping, struggling,
  Is He sure to bless?
"Angels, Prophets, Martyrs, Virgins,
      Answer Yes!"

XIX.

O HAPPY band of pilgrims,
    If onward ye will tread,
With JESUS as your Fellow,
    To JESUS as your Head!

O happy if ye labour
    As JESUS did for men,
O happy if ye hunger
    As JESUS hunger'd then!

The Cross that JESUS carried,
    He carried as your due:
The Crown that JESUS weareth,
    He weareth it for you.

The trials that beset you,
    The sorrows ye endure,
The manifold temptations
    That Death alone can cure,—

What are they but His jewels
    Of right celestial worth?
What are they but the ladder
    Set up to Heaven on earth?

O happy band of pilgrims
    Look upward to the skies,
Where such a light affliction
    Shall win you such a prize.

HYMNS.

XX.

LEAD, kindly Light, amid th' encircling gloom,
        Lead Thou me on!
The night is dark, and I am far from home —
        Lead Thou me on!
Keep Thou my feet; I do not ask to see
The distant scene, — one step's enough for me.

I was not ever thus, nor prayed that Thou
        Should'st lead me on;
I loved to choose and see my path; but now
        Lead Thou me on!
I loved the garish day, and spite of fears
Pride ruled my will: remember not past years.

So long Thy power hath bless'd me, sure it still
        Will lead me on,
O'er moor and fen, o'er crag and torrent, till
        The night is gone,
And with the morn those angel faces smile
Which I have loved long since, and lost awhile.

XXI.

WHY marvelling though the clouds be black,
    The path be rough to tread?
Why thus impatient for a track
    Of pleasure in its stead?

His path, on whom we fix our eye,
    Was never strewn with flowers;
How can we think on Calvary,
    And give one thought to ours?

And was the Cross so soft a bed,
    The Reed so fair a gem,
The Crown of Thorns that wreathed His Head
    So bright a diadem?

O who could bear to dwell at ease,
    Remembering what He bore?
O who would sigh for what might please,
    When He was tried so sore?

HYMNS.

The cross was borne by all the rest
  Of His elected Seed:
They clasped it bravely to their breast, —
  And why should we be freed?

Yea, in Thy Mercy, not Thy Wrath,
  Our trials Thou dost send;
Lest if we should not tread their path,
  We might not share its end.

Praise, in the Church's highest strain,
  To GOD the FATHER be;
And to the LAMB that once was slain
  And, HOLY GHOST, to Thee.

XXII.

THERE is a stream, whose waters rise
  Amidst the hills of Paradise,
Where foot of man hath never trod,
Proceeding from the Throne of GOD:
O give me sickness here, or strife,
So I may reach that spring of life!

There is a Rock that nigh at hand
Gives shadow in a weary land;
Who in that stricken Rock hath rest,
Finds water gushing from its breast:
O grant me, when this scene is o'er,
Their lot who thirst not any more.

There is a people who have cast
The strife and toil away at last:
On whom, — so calm their rest and sweet, —
The sun lights not nor any heat;
Give me with them at length to be,
And send me here what pleaseth Thee.

O Thou, who camest Death to spoil,
And barest weariness and toil;
And just before His chains were burst,
Fulfilling Scripture, saidst, "I thirst!"
Who call'st Thy weary servants o'er
The same rough road Thou trodd'st before;

HYMNS.

Thou Only Good! Thou Only Wise!
Who dost so lovingly chastise,
To give more strength, and add more grace, —
Grant me Thy Spirit to embrace,
The more, — the more that nature faints, —
The glorious portion of all Saints.

Thou wouldst not, Lord, ascend to reign,
But first on earth Thou sufferedst pain;
And now, O FATHER, at Thy side
For us He pleads, for us who died;
Shading from storm, and blast, and heat,
With that Eternal Paraclete.

FOR PENITENTS.

XXIII.

JESU, Name all names above,
  JESU, best and dearest,
JESU, Fount of perfect love;
  Holiest, tenderest, nearest;
JESU, source of grace completest,
JESU purest, JESU sweetest,
  JESU, well of power divine,
  Make me, keep me, seal me thine!

JESU, open me the gate
  That of old he enter'd
Who, in that most lost estate,
  Wholly on Thee ventur'd;
Thou, whose Wounds are ever pleading,
And Thy Passion interceding,
  From my misery let me rise
  To a Home in Paradise!

Thou didst call the Prodigal:
  Thou didst pardon Mary:
Thou whose Words can never fail,
  Love can never vary:
Lord, to heal my lost condition,
Give, — for Thou canst give, — contrition;
  Thou canst pardon all mine ill,
  If Thou wilt: O say, "I will!"

HYMNS.

Woe, that I have turn'd aside
  After fleshly pleasure!
Woe, that I have never tried
  For the Heavenly Treasure!
Treasures safe in Homes supernal,
Incorruptible, eternal!
  Treasure no less price hath won
  Than the Passion of the Son!

JESU, crown'd with thorns for me,
  Scourg'd for my transgression,
Witnessing through agony,
  That Thy good confession!
JESU, clad in purple raiment,
For my evils making payment,
  Let not all Thy woe and pain,
  Let not Calvary be in vain!

When I reach Death's bitter sea,
  And its waves roll higher,
Help the more forsaking me
  As the storm draws nigher:
JESU, leave me not to languish
Helpless, hopeless, full of anguish!
  Tell me, — " Verily I say,
  Thou shalt be with all to-day ! "

XXIV.

LOVING Shepherd, kind and true,
  Wilt Thou not in pity come
To Thy lamb? As shepherds do,
  Bear me in Thy bosom home;
Take me hence from earth's annoy
To Thy home of endless joy.

See how I have gone astray,
  In this earthly wilderness;
Come and take me soon away
  To Thy flock who dwell in bliss,
And Thy glory, Lord, behold,
Safe within Thy heavenly fold.

HYMNS.

For I fain would gaze on Thee,
  With the lambs to whom 'tis given
That they feed, from danger free,
  In the happy fields of heaven;
Praising Thee, all terrors o'er,
Never can they wander more.

Here I live in sore distress,
  Fearing, watching, hour by hour,
For my foes around me press,
  And I know their craft and power.
Lord, Thy lamb can never be
Safe one moment, but with Thee.

O Lord Jesus, let me not
  'Mid the ravening wolves e'er fall;
Help me as a shepherd ought,
  That I may escape them all;
Bear me homeward in Thy breast,
To Thy fold of endless rest.

XXV.

"I saw the Holy City, New Jerusalem, coming down from God, out of heaven, prepared as a bride adorned for her husband."

BLESSED city, heavenly Salem,
  Vision dear of peace and love,
Who of living stones art builded
  In the height of heaven above,
And, with angel hosts encircled,
  As a bride to earth dost move;

From celestial realms descending,
  Bridal glory round Thee shed,
Meet for Him whose love espoused thee,
  To thy Lord shalt thou be led;
All thy streets and all thy bulwarks,
  Of pure gold are fashioned.

Bright thy gates of pearl are shining,
  They are open evermore;
And by virtue of His merits
  Thither faithful souls do soar,

HYMNS.

Who for Christ's dear Name in this world
    Pain and tribulation bore.

Many a blow and biting sculpture
    Polished well those stones elect,
In their places now compacted
    By the heavenly Architect,
Who therewith hath willed for ever
    That His palace should be decked.

Praise and honour to the FATHER,
    Praise and honour to the SON,
Praise and honour to the SPIRIT,
    Ever Three and ever One,
One in might and One in glory,
    While eternal ages run.   Amen.

XXVI.

"Behold I lay in Sion a chief Corner-Stone, elect, precious."

CHRIST is made the sure foundation,
    CHRIST the Head and Corner-stone,
Chosen of the Lord, and precious,
    Binding all the Church in one,
Holy Sion's help for ever,
    And her confidence alone.

All that dedicated City,
    Dearly loved of GOD on high,
In exultant jubilation
    Pours perpetual melody:
GOD the One in Three adoring
    In glad hymns eternally.

To this Temple, where we call Thee,
    Come O Lord of Hosts to-day;
With Thy wonted loving-kindness,
    Hear Thy servants as they pray;
And Thy fullest benediction
    Shed within its walls alway.

Here vouchsafe to all Thy servants
    What they ask of Thee to gain,

What they gain from Thee for ever
  With the Blessed to retain,
And hereafter in Thy glory
  Evermore with Thee to reign.

Praise and honour to the FATHER,
  Praise and honour to the SON,
Praise and honour to the SPIRIT,
  Ever Three and ever One,
One in might and One in glory,
  While eternal ages run.   Amen.

XXVII.

" Unto you which believe He is precious."

JESU! the very thought is sweet!
  In that dear Name all heart-joys meet:
But oh! than honey sweeter far
The glimpses of His presence are.

No word is sung more sweet than this,
No sound is heard more full of bliss,
No thought brings sweeter comfort nigh,
Than JESUS, SON of GOD most High.

JESU, the hope of souls forlorn,
How good to them for sin that mourn!
To them that seek Thee, oh how kind!
But what art Thou to them that find?

No tongue of mortal can express,
No pen can write the blessedness,
He only who had proved it knows
What bliss from love of JESUS flows.

O Jesu, King of wondrous might!
O Victor, glorious from the fight!
Sweetness that may not be expressed,
And altogether loveliest!

Abide with us, O Lord, to-day,
Fulfil us with Thy grace, we pray;
And with Thine own True sweetness feed
Our souls, from sin and darkness freed.   Amen.

HYMNS.

XXVIII.

I.

"Here have we no continuing city, but we seek one to come."

Brief life is here our portion;
  Brief sorrow, short-lived care:
The life that knows no ending,
  The tearless life, is there.

O happy retribution!
  Short toil, eternal rest;
For mortals and for sinners
  A mansion with the blest.

That we should look, poor wand'rers,
  To have our Home on high!
That worms should seek for dwellings,
  Beyond the starry sky!

To all one happy guerdon,
  Of one celestial grace;
For all, for all, who mourn their fall,
  Is one eternal place:

And martyrdom hath roses
  Upon that heavenly ground:
And white and virgin lilies
  For virgin souls abound.

Then grief is turned to pleasure;
  Such pleasure, as below
No human voice can utter,
  No human heart can know:

And after fleshly scandal,
  And after this world's night,
And after storm and whirlwind,
  Is calm and joy and light.

And now we fight the battle,
  But then shall wear the crown
Of full and everlasting

And now we watch and struggle,
  And now we live in hope,
And Sion in her anguish
  With Babylon must cope;

But He whom now we trust in
  Shall then be seen and known;
And they that know and see Him
  Shall have Him for their own.

The morning shall awaken,
  The shadows shall decay,
And each true-hearted servant
  Shall shine as doth the day;

There GOD our KING and PORTION,
  In fullness of His grace,
Shall we behold for ever,
  And worship face to face.

II.

FOR thee, O dear, dear Country,
  Mine eyes their vigils keep;
For very love beholding
  Thy happy name they weep.

The mention of thy glory
  Is unction to the breast,
And medicine in sickness,
  And love and life and rest.

O one, O only mansion!
  O Paradise of joy!
Where tears are ever banished,
  And smiles have no alloy;

The Cross is all thy splendour;
  The Crucified thy praise;
His laud and benediction
  Thy ransomed people raise.

HYMNS.

The sardis and the topaz
  Unite in thee their rays;

Thine ageless walls are bonded
  With amethyst unpriced;
The saints build up its fabric,
  And the corner-stone is CHRIST.

Thou hast no shore, fair ocean!
  Thou hast no time, bright day!
Dear fountain of refreshment.
  To pilgrims far away!

Upon the Rock of Ages
  They raise thy holy tower;
Thine is the victor's laurel,
  And thine the golden dower.

III.

JERUSALEM the golden!
  With milk and honey blest;
Beneath thy contemplation
  Sink heart and voice opprest.

I know not, oh! I know not
  What joys await us there;
What radiancy of glory
  What bliss beyond compare.

They stand, those halls of Sion,
  All jubilant with song,
And bright with many an angel,
  And all the martyr throng.

The Prince is ever in them,
  The daylight is serene,
The pastures of the blessed
  Are decked in glorious sheen.

There is the throne of David;
  And there from care released,
The shout of them that triumph,
  The song of them that feast;

And they who with their Leader
　　Have conquered in the fight,
For ever and for ever
　　Are clad in robes of white.

O sweet and blessed country,
　　The Home of GOD's elect!
O sweet and blessed country,
　　That eager hearts expect!

JESU, in mercy bring us
　　To that dear land of rest;
Who art, with GOD the FATHER,
　　And SPIRIT ever blest.　Amen.

IV.

JERUSALEM the glorious!
　　The glory of the Elect!
O dear and future vision
　　That eager hearts expect:
Even now by faith I see Thee,
　　Even here Thy walls discern:
To Thee my thoughts are kindled,
　　And strive, and pant, and yearn.

Jerusalem, exulting
　　On that securest shore,
I hope Thee, wish Thee, sing Thee,
　　And love Thee evermore!
I ask not for my merit;
　　I seek not to deny
My merit is destruction,
　　A child of wrath am I.

But yet with faith I venture,
　　And hope, upon my way;
For those perennial guerdons
　　I labour night and day.
The best and dearest FATHER
　　Who made me, and who saved,
Bore with me in defilement,
　　And from defilement laved:—

HYMNS.

When in His strength I struggle,
  For very joy I leap,
When in my sin I totter,
  I weep, or try to weep:
And grace, sweet grace celestial,
  Shall all its love display,
And David's royal Fountain
  Purge every sin away.

O mine, my golden Syon!
  O lovelier far than gold!
With laurel-girt battalions,
  And safe victorious fold:
O sweet and blessed Country,
  Shall I ever see thy face?
O sweet and blessed Country,
  Shall I ever win thy grace?
I have the hope within me,
  To comfort and to bless!
Shall I ever win the prize itself?
  O tell me, tell me, yes!

Exult, O dust and ashes,
  The LORD shall be thy part:
His only, His for ever,
  Thou shalt be, and thou art!
Exult, O dust and ashes,
  The LORD shall be thy part:
His only, His for ever,
  Thou shalt be, and thou art!
            Amen.

DIES IRÆ.

XXIX.

I.

DAY of Vengeance, without morrow!
  Earth shall end in flame and sorrow,
As from saint and seer we borrow.

II.

Ah! what terror is impending,
When the Judge is seen descending,
And each secret veil is rending.

HYMNS.

III.

To the Throne, the trumpet sounding,
Through the sepulchres resounding
Summons all, with voice astounding.

IV.

Death and Nature, mazed, are quaking,
When, the grave's long slumber breaking,
Man to judgment is awaking.

V.

On the written volume's pages,
Life is shown in all its stages,
Judgment-record of past ages.

VI.

Sits the Judge, the raised arraigning,
Darkest mysteries explaining,
Nothing unavenged remaining.

VII.

What shall I then say, unfriended,
By no advocate attended,
When the just are scarce defended?

VIII.

King of majesty tremendous,
By Thy saving grace defend us;
Fount of pity, safety send us!

IX.

Holy JESUS, meek, forbearing,
For my sins the death-crown wearing,
Save me, in that day, despairing.

X.

Worn and weary Thou hast sought me;
By Thy Cross and Passion bought me,—
Spare the hope Thy labours brought me.

XI.

Righteous Judge of retribution,
Give, O give me absolution,
Ere the day of dissolution.

HYMNS.

XII.

As a guilty culprit groaning,
Flush'd my face, my errors owning,
Hear, O GOD, my spirit's moaning.

XIII.

Thou to Mary gav'st remission,
Heard'st the dying thief's petition,
Bad'st me hope in my contrition.

XIV.

In my prayers no grace discerning,
Yet on me Thy favour turning,
Save my soul from endless burning!

XV.

Give me, when Thy sheep confiding
Thou art from the goats dividing,
On Thy right a place abiding!

XVI.

When the wicked are confounded,
And by bitter flames surrounded,
Be my joyful pardon sounded!

XVII.

Prostrate, all my guilt discerning,
Heart as though to ashes turning,
Save, O save me from the burning! -

XVIII.

Day of weeping, when from ashes
Man shall rise 'mid lightning flashes,
Guilty, trembling with contrition,
Save him, FATHER, from perdition!
Holy JESU, Saviour Blest,
Grant him Thy Eternal Rest. Amen.

www.ingramcontent.com/pod-product-compliance
Lightning Source LLC
Chambersburg PA
CBHW030242170426
43202CB00009B/590